COSTUME of OLD TESTAMENT PEOPLES

PHILIP J WATSON

drawings by Jack Cassin-Scott

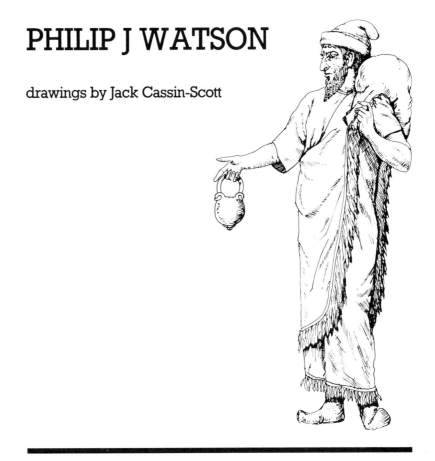

1987
CHELSEA HOUSE PUBLISHERS
NEW YORK · NEW HAVEN · PHILADELPHIA

© Philip J. Watson 1987
First published 1987

All rights reserved. No part of this publication
may be reproduced, in any form or by any
means, without permission from the Publisher

Printed in Great Britain by The Bath Press Ltd Bath

Published in the U.S.A. 1987 by Chelsea House Publishers
5014 West Chester Pike, Edgemont, PA 19028

Published in the U.K. by B T Batsford Limited
4 Fitzhardinge Street, London W1H 0AH

Library of Congress Cataloguing in Publication Data
Watson, Philip J.
    Costume of Old Testament Peoples
    Includes index.
    Summary: Outlines the geography and history of the area and
people covered. Describes the technology and materials associated
with ancient costume.

87–71085

ISBN 1–55546–770–9

Contents

Introduction 5

1 Setting the scene 6

2 Sumerians and Akkadians 10

3 The Babylonians 23

4 Amorites and Canaanites 30

5 Hittites and Arameans 35

6 Israelites and Phoenicians 44

7 The Assyrians 49

8 Elamites 59

Conclusion 63

Index 64

Bibliography

AKURGAL, E, *The Birth of Greek Art*, London 1968
AL-JADIR, W & AL-AZZAWI, D, *Assyrian Costumes and Jewelleries*, Baghdad 1970
FORBES, R J, *Studies in Ancient Technology*, vol IV, Leiden 1964 (Fabrics, weaving, etc)
FORBES, R J, *Studies in Ancient Technology*, vol V, Leiden 1966 (Leather)
FRANKFORT, H, *The Art and Architecture of the Ancient Orient*, Harmondsworth 1954
GURNEY, O, *The Hittites*, Harmondsworth 1964
HARDEN, D, *The Phoenicians*, Harmondsworth 1971
HODGES, H, *Technology in the Ancient World*
HOUSTON, M G, *Ancient Egyptian, Mesopotamian and Persian Costume and Decoration*, London 1954
MADHLOOM, T A, *The Chronology of Neo-Assyrian Art*, London 1970
MAXWELL-HYSLOP, K R, *Western Asiatic Jewellery* c *3000-612 BC*, London 1971
MOORTGAT, A, *The Art of Ancient Mesopotamia*, London 1969
PORADA, E, *Ancient Iran*, London 1965
READE, J E, *The Neo-Assyrian Court and Army: Evidence from the Sculptures*, 'Iraq' 34 (1972), 87-112
SINGER, C, HOLMYARD, E J, & HALL, A R (eds), *A History of Technology*, vol 1 chapter 16, 'Textiles, Basketry and
    Mats' by G M Crowfoot, Oxford 1968
WRIGHT, G E, *Biblical Archaeology*, London 1966
YADIN, Y, *The Art of Warfare in Biblical Lands*, London 1963

Introduction

The following pages provide an introductory survey of a large subject which has, unfortunately, been generally neglected both by students of the ancient world and by costume experts, as can readily be seen from a glance at the bibliography. However, detailed study of particular facets can produce results which are of importance not only for the history of costume but which also allow us to refine our understanding of the ancient civilizations.

The present work is based mainly on the pictorial evidence which survives from the ancient world in the form of statuary, relief sculpture and wall paintings. It is difficult, in many cases impossible, to marry up the evidence from ancient texts, which is considerable, with these pictorial representations.

The reader must also be aware of the shortcomings and dangers inherent in the pictorial record. Firstly the vast majority of evidence which has been preserved concerns royalty, nobility and officialdom, in other words 'the wealthy'. For the most part the dress of the common people probably varied and changed little and would have consisted of simpler garments made from poorer materials. This imbalance is naturally reflected in the pages of this volume. Secondly, the evidence available to us varies considerably, both in terms of quality and quantity, from one area to another. We have very little material from three thousand years of the Holy Land but so much from only three hundred years of Assyria that a monograph at least the size of the present book could be written on that alone. Finally a warning should be given against over-literal interpretation of the ancient sources. Allowance always has to be made for artistic conventions, stylizations, fossilizations and simple errors on the part of the artist. The ancients were after all only human despite the grandeur and romance which 'the mists of time' often seem to impart to the past.

CHRONOLOGICAL CHART

Date BC	Holy Land	North Syria	Central Turkey	Northern Iraq	Southern Iraq	Iran	Other World Events
3000		Sumerian influence			Sumerians Early Dynastic period	Early Elamite civilization	
2500					Akkadians Neo-Sumerian period		Pyramids built in Egypt
2000	Amorites Canaanites	Babylonian influence	Rise of Old Hittite kingdom	Old Assyrian kingdom	Old Babylonian period		Stonehenge
1500	Hittite empire INVASION OF SEA PEOPLES		Hittite empire	Middle Assyrian empire	Kassites	Classical or Middle Elamite period	Tomb of Tutankhamun in Egypt
1000	Israelites Assyrian empire	Aramean and neo-Hittite city states inland Phoenicians coast		Neo-Assyrian empire Fall of Assyria	Neo Babylon empire. Fall of Babylonia		
500 300 0	ALEXANDER THE GREAT					Achaemenid empire	

4

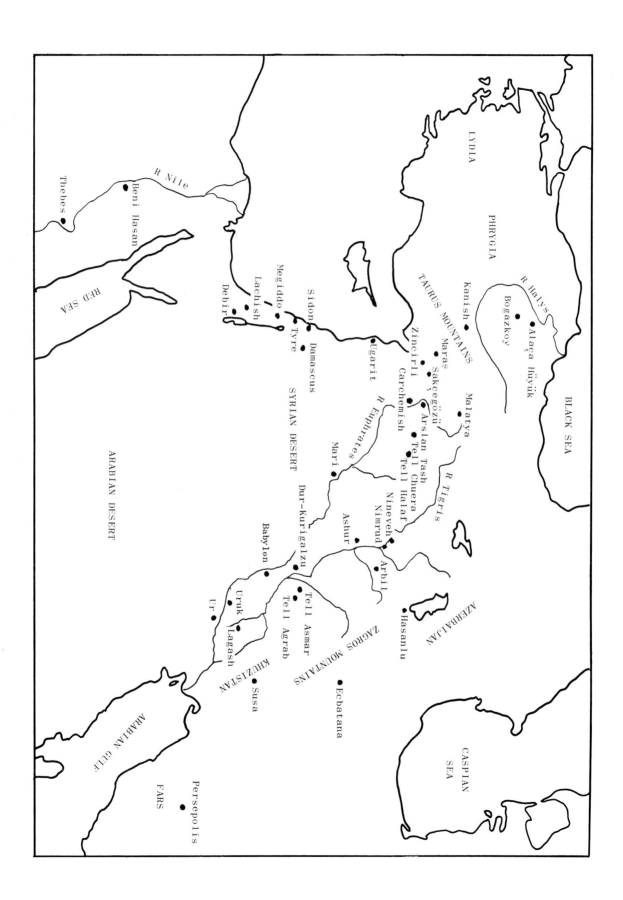

1 Setting the scene

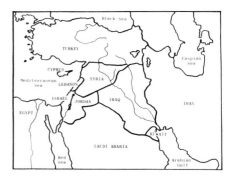

The Geographical area covered in this short volume is both large and varied encompassing as it does most of what we would today call the Middle East. In terms of modern frontiers this includes Iraq, Syria, Lebanon, Jordan, Israel, Turkey and Iran though of course in the past such political boundaries did not exist. Despite its size only a small part of this area is habitable and this is often referred to as the 'Fertile Crescent'. It comprises a broad crescent-shaped band of land running up the Syro-Palestinian coast in to northern Syria and southern Turkey before sweeping down along the courses of the rivers Euphrates and Tigris in Iraq. Between the two ends of the crescent lies the vast expanse of the Syrian desert, the northward extension of the Great Arabian desert.

Climatic factors obviously vary enormously, often very dramatically, over such a large area, In very broad terms the countries of the east Mediterranean coast have a fairly moderate climate with sufficient rainfall to support agriculture in many areas. The mountainous regions of southern Turkey, northern and eastern Iraq and western Iran however are very wet and very cold with many of the higher peaks retaining snow throughout the year. The Euphrates-Tigris plain, on the other hand, receives virtually no rainfall and irrigation is essential for agriculture with summer temperatures soaring to over 40° C; winter evenings can be frosty.

History

The history of the region is no less varied and displays the same dramatic contrasts especially during the period covered here, from about 3000 to 300 BC. Between the rivers Euphrates and Tigris there crystallized the world's first civilization, that of the Sumerians, inventors of, amongst other things, writing. This arose largely because of the politico-economic organization resulting from the necessity to manage 'co-operative' irrigation systems, essential for the production of food. Admixture of Semitic peoples from the desert and the west resulted in the ascendancy of first the Babylonians and then the Assyrians. The mountainous areas fringing the eastern and northern limits of the Fertile Crescent never produced civilizations by their very nature yet acted as refuge for tribes of, comparatively speaking, barbarian peoples who periodically descended on the cities of the plain, all too often with destructive results. In central Turkey a native civilization did flourish under the Hittite kings and at its apogee commanded a large area of southern Turkey and north west Syria.

Southern Syria and Palestine however never really progressed beyond achieving confederations of city-states whose territories were ever prey to the expansionist policies of Egyptian, Hittite, Assyrian, Babylonian, Persian, Greek and finally Roman imperial leaders. The Fertile Crescent is a region with no definite internal natural boundaries as a result of which there was a constant movement and intermixing of populations, settled and nomadic alike. The political scenario was in permanent flux and changes could take place gradually over centuries or might be precipitated by some single catastrophic event.

Sources

Archaeology provides us with three major sources of evidence for the ancient world. The **pictorial record**, preserved in the form of representational art, such as sculptures and wall paintings, is perhaps the most important from the point of view of costume study. Indeed this volume draws almost entirely on this source.

The second, that of the **written archives**, provides much valuable information though perhaps of more socio-economic interest. For example, many hundreds of Sumerian tablets have been preserved which record details of the manufacture of garments. These list the type of garment, the number of women employed in making it, the length of time taken, the type and quantities of materials used, the name of the supervisor and so on. Another valuable archive preserves records of the textile trade between the city of Ashur and a merchant colony in southern Turkey. Again the texts specify types of garments, quantity, weight, material, equivalent values in silver and the merchant's name together with many other valuable details. Genesis, amongst other sources, suggests that the origin of dress is associated with guilt and shamefulness and this is reflected in the pictorial record where children normally go naked until puberty (ie whilst they are 'innocent') and prisoners are often stripped as the final humiliation following defeat. Fascinating as these details are however there is hardly a place for them in a book such as this if only because as yet it is virtually impossible to match the written record with the pictorial. Although there are many tens of words for different types of garments in the Sumerian and Akkadian languages we cannot as yet assign these with any confidence to the pictorial representations of clothes which we find in the sculptures.

The third source is what archaeologists usually term the 'material remains', generally speaking the things which were left behind on abandonment of a site, the rubbish which was thrown away, the equipment buried with the dead, buildings, structures and so on. For example, spindle whorls are found on most sites telling us that spinning of wool was practised by the people who lived there. The earliest of these date back to prehistoric times. Examination of animal bones tell us that sheep and goats were herded by these early spinning communities. Loom weights and impressions of woven cloth in clay or adhering to metal artefacts tell us that weaving was known. Excavations at the site of Debir for example have shown that it was an important weaving and dyeing centre. It has yielded massive quantities of loom weights and many buildings with rooms containing two large dye vats.

Materials and technology

Before describing the costume of the ancient near eastern peoples it is useful to give a brief survey of the materials which were available to them. One of the oldest of these was leather, used at first as simple hides either with or without the fleece left on. We know from texts that tanners and leatherworkers were an important body of craftsmen from Sumerian times onwards and in Babylonia around 1800 BC it was certainly not unusual for private individuals to buy themselves a pair of leather sandals. Tanners are also mentioned in the Old Testament where they are somewhat despised because of the smell of their trade, and tanneries had to be situated on the leeward (ie down wind) side of towns and at some distance away.

Wool was especially important in Sumer, Babylonia and Assyria and vast flocks of sheep and goats were herded. There is also occasional mention of utilizing the wool of wild goats and ibex. At first the wool was obtained by plucking or combing but in later times it was shorn. The texts mention various types and qualities of wool, some of them used for special garments others of general purpose, though it is not possible to relate these details to the depictions of actual costumes.

Flax, from which linen is made, was also known in Mesopotamia at least from neo-Sumerian times, though it was always overshadowed there by the importance and abundance of wool which was used for every day dress and that of commoners. Linen garments were very much a luxury item, used for example to drape the images of gods. Syria and Palestine however had a reputation for producing good quality flax, and fine linen garments were amongst the tribute which the Assyrian kings brought back from their campaigns there. Again the texts inform us of various types and qualities of linen though the meanings of many of these terms can only be arrived at by 'educated guesswork'.

Cotton played virtually no part in the period covered by this book. It was not introduced into Mesopotamia until the seventh century BC when king Sennacherib imported some cotton plants, probably from India, to plant in his royal gardens. Silk arrived in the area even later, via Persia.

Spinning, be it of wool or flax, was essentially a female occupation throughout the area and at all periods (figure 1). The idea of spinning probably arose from simple hand spinning, rolling the fibres between the hands or between hand and thigh and then twisting the resultant thread. From a very early period however spindles were used, usually nothing more than a stick about 30 cm long with a whorl, a disc- or cone-shaped piece of clay, pottery, stone, bone or wood perforated through the middle and fitted to one or other end. Many studies have been carried out to determine the type of loom(s) which might have been used by the ancient weavers and the scanty remains of fabrics have been examined by textile experts to assess the weaver's art. Felting is one of the oldest textile crafts which entails simply pressing, rolling and beating the fibres (usually wool or other animal hair) into a matted fabric of even texture.

Dyeing of the finished materials, either as thread or cloth, was carried out using a variety of vegetable dyes which yielded mainly reds, blues, purples and yellows. There was of course also the natural off-whites, browns and blacks of the wool itself. The tradition of dyeing using the *Murex*-shell, so-called Phoenician purple, is discussed further below.

Several of the techniques of the ancient textile worker are described in the companion volume on Egyptian costume and the reader who requires further information can consult the excellent volumes on ancient technology which are listed in the bibliography.

1   A noble lady spinning. From a fragment of relief from Elam
c 1000 BC

2 Sumerians and Akkadians

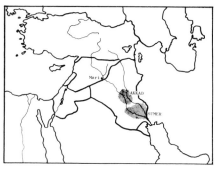

Early Dynastic	3000-2400 BC
Old Akkadian	2400-2200 BC
Neo-Sumerian	2100-2000 BC

The Sumerians occupied the area between the rivers Euphrates and Tigris in southern Iraq. The earliest permanent settlements date to about 5000 BC. Even at this early period their economy was based on agriculture using artificial irrigation and by about 3200 BC they had begun to use a system of writing. These early achievements culminated in a series of powerful city-states which represent the classical era of Sumerian civilization, the Early dynastic period (c. 3000-2370 BC). This ended when Sargon I, a Semite, took control of the city-states and imposed political unity on Sumer. The ensuing Old Akkadian period (2370-2230 BC) was itself brought to an end by an influx of mountain people from the foothills of the Zagros. After a rather confused century the Sumerians rallied under the leadership of the city of Ur to produce a somewhat hybrid neo-Sumerian phase (2130-2021 BC).

Some of the earliest depictions of garments from Mesopotamia, indeed from anywhere in the world, are those on the Uruk vase dating to the early third millennium BC. This is a cult vessel made of alabaster. It has three registers of relief decoration showing a procession of sacrificial animals and offering bearers led by a man who approaches a female figure standing before a shrine. This scene probably depicts the goddess Inanna (or her high priestess) receiving her bridegroom Dumuzi on New Year's Day to celebrate the sacred marriage. Whether it is a depiction of the mythical event itself or of a ceremony which took place every New Year's Day need not concern us here. What we should note is that the goddess or priestess is wearing a long cloak with a border down one edge and along the bottom (figure 2). The bridegroom, approaching her is badly damaged but appears to wear a garment made from transparent netting. He has two assistants wearing short, knee-length, wrap-round kilts, again . with borders at one edge and the bottom. One of them is presenting a cloth girdle with tasselled ends (figure 3). The remaining offering bearers are all naked.

The dress of the main male figure can be parallelled on an incised plaque in the Louvre where a male figure wears a long net skirt with a fringed border (figure 4). His head-dress consists of two leaf-shaped pieces with herring-bone pattern, which probably have no connection wtih feathers but rather represent a vegetation aspect of Sumerian religion, possibly the god Ningirsu or his high priest.

2 The goddess Inanna or her high priestess as depicted on the Uruk vase

Early Dynastic Sumer

Books normally show the Sumerians wearing sheepskin kilts either with fleece left on or plucked to give a bare leather skirt. If we contrast this with Sumerian achievements in other fields of arts and crafts, especially metalworking and pottery, it appears a very primitive costume indeed. However, wool spinning was known from earliest times and impressions of woven fabrics have been found from these early periods. Therefore Sumerian garments, whilst possibly made from sheepskin, may just as likely have been from a woven fabric in which long loops of wool were used to give the characteristic shaggy appearance. If sheepskins were used they must have been combed and trimmed in various ways to produce the patterns shown on the statues.

Whatever the material, certainly the Sumerian figures of the Early Dynastic period are shown wearing skirts which characteristically, though not always, have a shaggy appearance. For example, on the Standard of Ur which apparently celebrates a military victory and was found in a grave at the royal cemetery of Ur, figures of shell inlaid into bitumen are shown wearing smooth calf-length skirts, the bottom hems of which have been cut to produce fringes. They are held up by thick padded belts or girdles, usually plain and somehow tied at the back to leave a small piece dangling down (figure 5). The same type of skirt is worn by the officials participating in the banquet, the figures serving them, the men bringing in the tribute, a harpist and a female singer. Only the king is shown wearing a shaggy skirt.

3 A tribute bearer from the Uruk vase presenting a tasselled girdle to the goddess

◀4 Male figure wearing a long net skirt. From a limestone relief plaque from Lagash

5 A figure from the banqueting ▶ scene on the Standard of Ur

11

Other figures wear what is obviously a wrap-round kilt open at one side and which in profile does not have a straight hem but one with an inverted V-shape (figure 6). These kilts also appear to be supported by a belt. They are closer fitting, shorter, have less pronounced fringing and are almost certainly of woven material rather than being skins.

Yet other figures on the standard wear a smooth skirt but with an extra piece which is brought around the back and up over the left shoulder (figure 7).

Finally there are spearmen who wear a smooth, fringed skirt though, at knee-length, it is shorter than that worn by the others. In addition they wear a mantle, tied at the neck but otherwise open down the front; this was perhaps made from a type of felt and had metal studs set in it (figure 8). As head protection they wear close fitting helmets, slightly pointed on top, with chin straps to secure them. These were probably made of leather though metal helmets were certainly known later.

Everyone is shown clean-shaven and bald except for one man leading in a goat who has black hair and a short square black beard, and the songstress who is shown with shoulder-length hair pulled back behind her ears. All the figures are barefoot and, except for the spearmen, bare-chested. The sash across the harpist's chest is a strap to support his instrument as the cross hatched decoration on it is also found around the bull's head on the harp.

6   A figure from the tribute parade on the Standard of Ur

7   A figure from the Standard of Ur wearing a skirt with shoulder piece

8   One of the spearmen from the Standard of Ur

Men's dress

We have already seen a certain variety amongst the skirts shown on the Standard of Ur. From other pieces which have survived, mainly statues, statuettes and relief plaques, we can expand this picture. The simple skirt could be worn either ankle-, mid-calf or knee-length. We have already discussed the question as to whether these skirts were made from skins either with or without fleece or from a shaggy-piled woven material. Be that as it may, there is certainly variation in the method of trimming or style of weaving whichever the case may be. For example, skirts are found which are plain except for a fringe at the bottom. These are often worn by soldiers and servants (figure 9). Commonest on statues are those which are shaggy all over but these were probably more or less restricted to use by royalty. They were usually trimmed and tiered to imitate a series of between three and seven flounces. Some statues show a tail-like piece of material hanging down from the left hand side of the waistband at the back (figure 10). Finally a more elaborate skirt appears to be decorated with short tufts on its upper parts and longer tufts for its fringe. Two slightly longer pieces hang down from the plain, padded belt, one each side (figure 11).

◀ 9   Man, possibly a temple servant; based on a figurine from Tell Asmar

11   Rear view of a figure wearing a skirt with variable length tufts and two pieces hanging from the belt

10a   Man wearing a long shaggy skirt; based on a statuette from Assur

10b   Rear view of skirt showing the tail like piece of material hanging from the belt; based on a statuette of a son of Eannatum, ruler of Lagash

Short knee-length skirts are worn by figures on a plaque from Ur which consist of a single row of long tufts giving them a pleated appearance (figure 12). They have a plain flap of material at centre front in the shape of an inverted triangle. Whether this is merely a decorative addition or is intended to conceal the slit of a wrap round kilt can only be guessed. Note however that the garment has a horizontal hem line suggesting a skirt rather than a kilt which is normally shown with an angled hem line.

On his victory stela, the so-called 'Stela of Vultures', Eannatum the ruler of Lagash is shown at the head of his army wearing the expected shaggy skirt but in addition he has a large woollen shawl thrown obliquely across his left shoulder and coming down under his right arm.

Women's dress

We have already seen a songstress on the Standard of Ur, wearing the simple skirt. It was more usual however, especially for royal ladies, to have garments which covered the chest. The simplest of these is a form of the skirt which has an extra length of material brought around the back and thrown up and over the left shoulder but leaving the right breast bare (figure 13).

12   Figure in a short kilt with triangular flap at the front; from a votive plaque from Ur

(a)

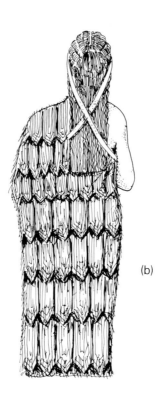

(b)

13   A woman from Lagash

14

More common still was a form of cloak which passed under the right armpit, round the back and over the left shoulder and left arm covering both breasts (figure 14). It was probably secured by a pin, many examples of which are known from the Early Dynastic period though none of the statues actually depict such a method of fastening. As with skirts examples are found which are plain all over, plain with a fringe at the bottom or shaggy all over.

A cloak which has pieces drawn up over both shoulders is found much more rarely (see below figure 23).

Male hairstyles and headgear

Men are commonly depicted clean shaven and with bare shaved heads. Many statuettes of male figures have been found however, perhaps representing temple personnel, which are shown with long, square-ended rectangular beards. They also have long hair or wigs parted down the centre and hanging down each side of the face on to the chest usually stopping level with the end of the beard (figure 9). Long rectangular beards could also be worn with much shorter, close cropped hair (figure 15). A shaved head with short close cropped beard is found on a figure from Ashur (figure 10a).

Leather helmets have already been seen on the heads of soldiers on the Standard of Ur and similar helmets are worn by the troops on the Stela of Vultures. These however lack the chinstrap (figure 16a). Eannatum himself wears a similar but more elaborate helmet (figure 16b). Identical in shape it is distinguished by having a moulded ear and head band holding up an imitation chignon. That this is not Eannatum's actual ear and hair is obvious as his real hair is shown spreading over his shoulder from beneath the back of the helmet. This type of moulded decoration must surely indicate that the helmet was made of metal, not leather, and the same must be postulated for those of the troops in view of the similar overall shape.

14 A woman in typical Early Dynastic dress

15 Hair and beard as depicted on a limestone foundation figurine

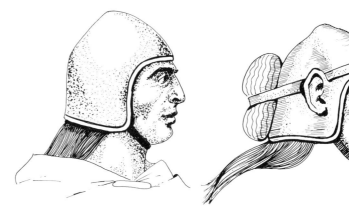

16a A soldier's helmet as shown on Eannatum's Stela of the Vultures

16b More elaborate royal helmet as depicted on the same stela

That such elaborate metal helmets did exist is known from the cult headdress of Meskalamdug from Ur which is made of gold (figure 17). This is moulded and engraved to depict both the ears and an elaborate hair-do with chignon secured by a head band. Inside was padded with cloth fastened to the outside through the holes which run around the bottom edge.

Female hairstyles and headgear

Generally speaking the women are shown with a variety of hairstyles and headdress. Hair could be worn short or long. Short hair for example could be back-combed or combed upwards and fluffed out whilst long hair was tied into a pony tail by means of a head band which crossed over at the back to secure the bunch of hair (figure 13). A variety of turban-like hats are found ranging from simple forms to the finely pleated bonnet on a head from Tell Agrab (figure 18).

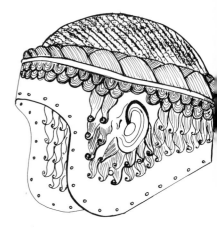

17   The golden helmet of Meskalamdug found in a tomb at Ur

Early Dynastic Mari and Tell Chuera

Syria, especially north-east Syria, was under largely Sumerian influence at this period and the costume reflects essentially Sumerian traditions.

Many pieces of sculpture have been unearthed amongst the ruins at Mari on the upper Euphrates and these, at least in terms of their dress, are little different from those of mainstream Sumer. It is only in the finer detail of sculptural style and perhaps a tendency towards a more naturalistic 'portrait' which distinguishes them as being of a different school. Similar remarks apply to the statues from Tell Chuera, though as yet they form a much smaller group.

Men's dress

The long ankle-length shaggy or long-tufted skirt is the commonest form of dress found on the male figures. Also found is the shaggy skirt with a piece brought up and thrown over the left shoulder (figure 19). The figures from Tell Chuera resemble the 'temple personnel' figures from Tell Asmar and wear calf-length skirts, plain above with a tufted fringe along the bottom hem. A short piece projects from beneath the padded waistband and hangs down at the rear left side (figure 20).

Women's dress

Likewise the women exhibit a range of garments in Sumerian style. The seated statue of the singer Ur-Nanshe wears, like the songstress on the Standard of Ur, a skirt only. There is some indication of a shaggy pile over her knees and there is a 'tail' hanging down at the back from the waistband (figure 21). Another seated figure (figure 22) also wears a shaggy skirt though her torso is missing and it is not known whether she was also bare breasted. However in addition to the skirt she wears a shaggy mantle of obviously the same material but with a tasselled edge. This is draped down her back and pulled up over her head. Equally parallel with Sumerian

18   Woman's pleated bonnet or turban; from a figure from Tell Agrab

19   King Lamgi-Mari of Mari

20   Rear view of a figure from Tell Chuera, very much reminiscent of the temple personnel figures from Tell Asmar

21   The songstress Ur-Nanshe from Mari

22   Figure of a woman from Mari

23   A woman from Mari wearing the cloak which had pieces brought up over both shoulders

16

styles are a cloak, plain but for fringes down one edge and along the bottom hem, which is worn under the right armpit but over the left shoulder and the cloak with pieces brought up and over both shoulders to hang down over the arms; the example illustrated here is of shaggy material (figure 23).

19

21

23

20

22

Men's hair

Again fashions reflect the situation in Sumer. Men are seen with bald heads and clean shaven chins, shaved heads with short beards and shaved heads with long tapering beards (figure 24). The statuette of king Lamgi-Mari (figure 19) has the elaborate hairstyle bunched into a chignon and secured by a head band as seen on the helmet worn by Eannatum on the Stela of Vultures and on the golden helmet of Meskalamdug. The figures from Tell Chuera have long rectangular beards and centrally parted hair hanging over the shoulders to the same level as the beard.

24

Women's hair

The simplest style is found on the singer Ur-Nanshe whose hair is tucked behind her ears and combed back over her shoulder. It is straight initially then waved and curled at the ends (figure 21). The hair of the remaining women from Mari is concealed by a variety of headdresses and appears merely as a fringe over their foreheads. Their headgear resemble felt hats usually curved and wider at the top with projections to either side at the level of the ears (figure 23, 25 and 26).

The Old Akkadian and Neo-Sumerian Periods

With the Old Akkadian period there is a noticeable change in costume or at least in the depiction of it. The shaggy skirts of either fleeces or piled material of the Early Dynastic era are replaced by clothes of an obviously more finely woven material and one which was much thinner. This is reflected in the way clothes are much closer fitting. On the one hand they hug the contours of shoulders and chest so that on the finest sculptures details of the muscles can be seen 'through' the garment. On the other hand they hang in a loose, draped fashion rather than in the stiff and solid manner seen in the Early Dynastic clothes.

25

The Old Akkadian and neo-Sumerian periods are really indistinguishable in terms of fashion. The Old Akkadian pieces tend to be finer with the neo-Sumerian ones having a somewhat fossilized and tired appearance though this probably reflects trends in sculpture rather than any marked change in the fashion of clothes.

Men's dress

The normal male garment in this period appears to have consisted of a single, rectangular piece of material draped around the body to produce a fairly tight-fitting gown, at least on the upper parts. An early example is seen on statues of Manishtusu where the material has been wrapped around the body, thrown over the left shoulder, the upper edge rolled into a pad around the waist and tucked in at the back. It is made from a finely woven material with a short fringed border along the selvedge and tassels on the warp end.

26

In his many statues, Gudea, ruler of Lagash, is also shown wearing a similar shawl-like garment but draped in a slightly different manner (figure 27). Gudea's robe appears to have been taken from the left armpit around the back and front of the body then again round the back before being thrown upwards across the chest and over the left shoulder coming once more around the back and tucking in under the right armpit. Movement of the left arm would have been considerably restricted by this garment. Although essentially a rectangular piece of material such garments appear on occasions to have had at least one edge shaped (figure 28a). Few statues of the neo-Sumerian kings survive.

Another garment, worn by gods and the king on ceremonial occasions reflects the earlier shaggy cloaks in its style. It consists of a fairly loose cylindrical garment draped over the left arm and shoulder but passing under the right armpit leaving the right shoulder exposed. Its similarity to the women's cloaks of the Early Dynastic period is immediately apparent. The garment consists of a series of flounces of equal length with a simple border at the top perhaps representing a turned over edge (figure 28b).

24 Long tapering beards such as this were quite commonly worn by the men of Mari

25 A lady from Mari wearing a tall hat with projections behind the ears

26 A ladies felt hat from Mari

27 Statuette of Gudea, ruler of Lagash. The change in style from the Early Dynastic period is immediately apparent

28a Gudea wearing a draped robe with one edge fringed and shaped being led by a divinity in flounced dress (figure 28b)

(a)

(b)

The third major male garment of this period is normally worn by soldiers including the king on military expeditions. It consists of a wrap-over kilt or skirt with a fringe down the vertical edge. In addition a piece of material is thrown obliquely across the chest sash-like coming down the back with the two ends tied in a simple knot above the right hip (figure 29). On other figures this was worn more in the fashion of a scarf going around the shoulders and crossing on the chest (figure 30).

32   Lady in a finely draped robe probably consisting of a single rectangular piece of material   ▶

29   Military kilt as worn by king
◀ Naram-Sin on his Victory Stela

30   Figure wearing a scarf like sash and a helmet with flexible neck guard

Women's dress

Depictions of women from this period are few but two major styles of garments appear to have been in vogue, both reflecting earlier traditions. One is the flounced cloak-like garment already described above as worn by gods and kings on religious occasions. An identical garment was also worn by goddesses and high priestesses. In addition flounced dresses with round necks are shown worn over both shoulders (figure 31).

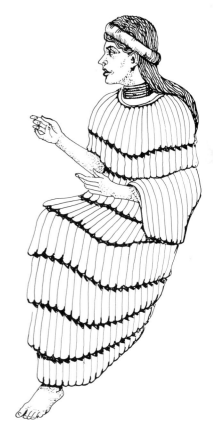

31   A goddess in a flounced dress with round neck; note that it is worn over both shoulders

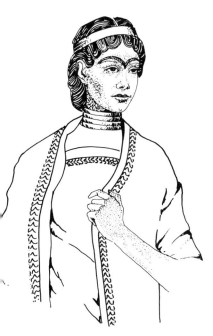

The second is probably a single piece of material as was the man's drape in this period but it was worn so that it came over both shoulders and appeared symmetrical from the front (figure 32). A method for draping such a garment has been suggested whereby the centre of the top edge is placed against the centre of the chest. The two sides are taken round the back, crossing over so that the left side is underneath and the corners are then thrown over the shoulders. On the example illustrated here the material has a decorative, perhaps embroidered, border.

Men's hair and headgear

Gudea is normally depicted clean shaven though other figures wear beards, usually pointed (figure 29) and sometimes curled (figure 30). Gods are shown with rectangular beards (figure 28b). An elaborate hairstyle is portrayed on the life-size bronze head of a king, possibly Naram-Sin (figure 33). The hair is parted down the middle and combed into a series of segments over the forehead with plaits of hair from the sides wound round the head tapering towards the front. A flat fillet, probably a metal band, helps to hold this in place. At the back the hair is plaited and drawn up into a heavy chignon. The pointed beard exhibits three styles of curl.

A less elaborate style consists of wavy hair combed so as to radiate from a point on the centre of the head and then cut to an equal length all round to produce a 'pudding basin' effect (figure 34). It is possible however that it represents a cap or some form of hair net rather than the hair itself. Certainly other figures, especially Gudea, are shown in similar style but with the addition of a wide, thick band all round the head which must surely indicate a woollen cap or turban of some form (figure 35). The conventionalized decoration could represent either curls or a decorated fabric.

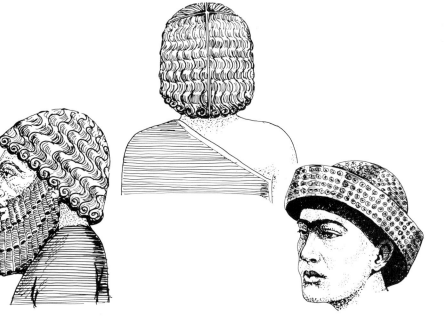

33   Head of an Akkadian king, possibly Naram-Sin

34   Figure with 'pudding-basin' ▶ haircut

35   Head of Gudea with a wide band around his head, possibly the brim of a close fitting cloth hat

Other headgear ranges from simple conical hats to the elaborate creations worn by the gods (figure 28b) consisting of hats embellished with horns symbolizing divinity with a sphere on top worn over chignoned hair.

Military helmets are worn by the king and his soldiers. The former's is pointed, has a neck guard and is decorated with horns (figure 29). The soldier's helmet (figure 30) likewise has a neck guard and from the apparent flexibility of this it must surely have been made of leather, not metal.

Women's hair and headgear

The simplest style is long hair combed straight, swept back over the shoulders and held in place by a head band (figure 31). More commonly a woman's hair was drawn up into a chignon again held in place by a head band. Priestesses could have ringlets descending down the front of their ears from beneath a thick headband or turban. Thin smooth caps resembling hair nets were probably not uncommon.

Footwear

There is remarkably little evidence for footwear from the early sculptures. Naram-Sin on the Victory Stela is shown wearing sandals made from leather strips (figure 29) and these were probably more widespread than the sculptures would have us believe. Many of the statues which have survived had religious significance and the subjects were doubtless shown barefoot out of respect to the divinity.

Mari in the Old Akkadian and Neo-Sumerian Periods

The statues of the *šakkanakku* or governors of Mari from these periods again reflect Mesopotamian customs. The main garment consists essentially of a drape with simple fringed borders or more complicated tasselled and fringed edges. Long elaborately curled beards and close fitting caps with a thickened band also imitate Mesopotamian prototypes (figures 36-38).

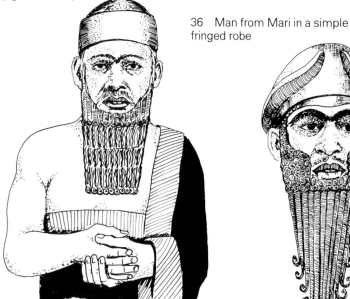

36 Man from Mari in a simple fringed robe

37 Idi-ilum of Mari showing front and back of his elaborately tasselled drape

38 Puzur-Ishtar of Mari sporting an enviable long tapering beard.

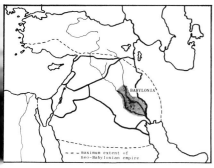

Old Babylonian	1800-1600 BC
Kassites	1400-1100 BC
Neo Babylonian	625- 539 BC

3 The Babylonians

The Babylonians are not to be regarded as an ethnic group. The term is rather a politico-historical convenience to designate the civilization of southern Iraq from about 1800 BC onwards which had the city of Babylon as its capital. It was governed by a dynasty of Semitic kings who formed a ruling elite over the population which was basically the traditional Sumero-Akkadian stock with some Semitic infiltration from the Amorite nomads.

Old Babylonian costume (1792-1595 BC) effectively continues the fashion established in the Old Akkadian and neo-Sumerian periods. Hammurapi for example is shown on his law code stela (figure 39) dressed in the familiar draped robe with a pudding-basin brimmed hat standing before a seated god wearing the equally familiar flounced cloak and multiple horn headdress.

39 The top of the stela containing Hammurapi's law code showing the king in a typical Old Babylonian robe before a seated god in a flounced dress

Gods and goddesses are often shown in the Old Babylonian period wearing a long slit skirt or dress though this has more the nature of a long cape or apron as in some instances the figure wears a conventional short skirt or kilt beneath it (figure 40), whilst in others the figures are naked beneath (figure 41). Characteristically dressed water goddesses are also found in the Old Babylonian period (see page 29).

The Kassites

Babylon was overthrown by the Hittite king Mursilis in 1595 BC and thereafter it was ruled by a group of people known as Kassites. The Kassites were Indo-Europeans who descended on Babylonia from the eastern Zagros Mountains and their origins are to be found to the east of Mesopotamia in or beyond Iran. Little of their art has survived but two genres are important from the point of view of portraying costume. There are some wall paintings, known mainly from the palace at Dur-Kurigalzu, and *kudurru*, or boundary stones, stone stelae inscribed with texts recording royal grants of land and often decorated with scenes carved in relief.

The paintings at Dur-Kurigalzu contain two principal classes of figures. Some are shown bare-headed and wear long robes; a head band secures long hair which hangs down their backs and they have long beards. Secondly, there is a more imposing figure with a shorter beard but equally long hair wearing a tunic with short sleeves and a belt or girdle around the waist. Across the front is a sash with fringes and the figure wears a fez-like hat tapering towards the top which is flat (figure 42).

40

40 Figure wearing a long slit skirt over a short kilt; from a terra cotta relief plaque

41 A goddess dressed in only a slit cape

41

The boundary stones are most important for the legal and historical significance of the texts with which they are inscribed though the reliefs abound with religious symbols and symbolism much of which is still not clearly understood. Many of these scenes, being of a religious character, tend to contain fossilized elements, survivals from the previous iconography, and are not relevant to this study. For example one commonly encounters divinities dressed in the now familiar flounced cloaks and divine heroes and warriors in the short military kilts of previous eras. At least one stone stands out however as reflecting a more secular nature. It is that which records a grant of land by king Melishipak (1188-1174) to his daughter and the scene of the *kudurru* possibly records the act of granting the land itself (figure 43). In it Melishipak is shown leading his daughter before the goddess Nana and the costume probably reflects that of the time. The goddess is wearing a flounced robe, though perhaps of finer quality than in the past. Likewise her hair with the heavy chignon is familiar enough. Her headgear however is new and takes the form of a very square crown with two girdling bands and decorated at the top with feathers or veined leaves. The king is wearing a long short-sleeved tunic with a scarf-like sash around his neck and crossing over on his chest. The garment has a fringed border along the bottom and is given some shape by the addition of a waist band. He wears a somewhat floppy, perhaps felt, pointed hat atop his long curled hair and beard. His daughter is dressed in a garment recalling more the drapes of earlier periods but more elaborately arranged. In addition to fringed edges the bottom hem has a border of embroidered or applied rosettes.

42

42   A Kassite as depicted in the wall paintings at the palace of Dur-Kuriglazu

43   The *kudurru* or boundary stone of king Melishipak

25

The Neo-Babylonian Era

After the Kassite period Babylonia fell under the political influence and dominance of Assyria to a greater or lesser extent. The boundary stelae from the later periods depict figures wearing similar garments. For example the stela of Marduk-nadin-akhhe (1098-1081) shows the king dressed in a very elaborately embroidered tunic with long sleeves (figure 44). He wears an equally ornate waistband but a plain thin sash forming an X across his chest. His hat is almost identical to that worn by the goddess Nana on the *kudurru* of Melishipak, even down to the row of feather or leaf decoration along the top edge, but has additionally a pointed centre boss on top. On his feet are a pair of thin slippers or stockings perhaps made from a net-like material.

A later *kudurru* of king Marduk-apla-iddina (Merodach-Baladan) II (721-720) shows the king dressed more after the fashion of Melishipak (figure 45). He wears a relatively plain though well cut tunic with elbow length sleeves and a plain, narrow crossed sash. From the rear of the waistband there appear to hang several thin strips of material or a pleated back-apron; however, it may be that the back of the tunic itself was gathered and pleated despite the difference in length between the pleated area and the rest of the tunic. A long ribbon hangs from his pointed hat and his feet are stockinged or slippered.

44   From the boundary stone of Marduknadinakhe showing him in an elaborately embroidered tunic

45   From the *kudurru* of Marduk-aplaiddina

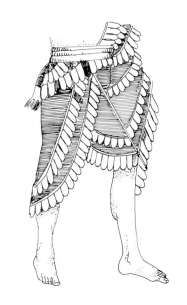

Mari in the Old Babylonian Period

With the Old Babylonian period, possibly a little before, a new style of garment appears at Mari best illustrated in the wall paintings from various rooms of the palace. Several fragments of painting have been found depicting men leading bulls, presumably sacrificial animals being led to slaughter. The figures leading the bulls are dressed in knee-length kilts adorned with fringed material (figure 46). Whether this fringed material is part of the fabric of the kilt, was attached to the kilt or was simply wrapped around the body independently is uncertain. It is difficult to envisage what the material or garment would have looked like if the fringing were part of it and on the basis of this and the fact that the fringed material is thrown up over the shoulder most commentators favour the latter hypothesis. However there is a certain overall resemblance to the Early Dynastic skirts with an extra piece brought over the shoulder and it may ultimately be necessary to make allowance for differing artistic conventions. Despite this possibility the garments do present a distinctive aspect which can only be due to west semitic influences. The kilts are supported by a triple girdle from which are suspended lotus blossoms. A variety of hats are worn; there is a simple domed version (figure 47) and one of obviously softer material with a head band (figure 48).

46 One of the figures leading bulls from the wall paintings in the palace at Mari; he is dressed in a kilt embellished with strips of fringed material

47 Domed hat on a figure from the Mari wall paintings

48 A floppy hat from the same source

Another painting, the so-called 'Investiture of Zimri-Lim', depicts the king similarly wearing a short kilt draped over with fringed material giving the appearance of a long cloak or cape (figure 49). He is standing before a goddess wearing a long slit skirt over a knee-length tunic with short sleeves and the crossed sash which we have seen became popular in the Kassite period. The long slit skirt, which we have already encountered in Babylonia itself, possibly gave rise to the back apron, if such it is, seen on the *kudurru* of Marduk-apla-iddina. The Investiture of Zimri-Lim also depicts a god in a diagonally cut kilt similar to those worn by the figures leading bulls, divinities in traditional Mesopotamian flounced dresses and

49 Part of the so-called 'Investiture of Zimri-Lim' scene showing several garments in contemporary use

water goddesses in long 'flowing' gowns. A good example of this type of dress can be seen on a statue of a water goddess from Mari (figure 50). Ostensibly she wears a typical flounced dress but many of its details, as in the kilted bull leaders, appear alien to Mesopotamian traditions such as the diagonally cut bodice with its short fringed sleeves. The dress itself is decorated with vertical wavy lines suggesting waves or ripples of water and ending in volutes at the hem. This treatment can be found on other depictions of water goddesses but a quaint additional detail to this piece are the fish swimming amongst the skirt. The figure wears accessories in the form of a multiple strand necklace, several bangles and head piece with two curving horns over a rather heavy hairstyle.

50   A finely dressed water goddess
from Mari

4 Amorites and Canaanites

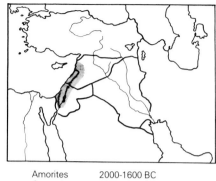

Amorites	2000-1600 BC
Canaanites	1500-1200 BC

Our knowledge of the dress of the Biblical area itself is less than that for Mesopotamia as we lack both wealth of archaeological finds and textual material. Although finds of everyday culture are almost as frequent as in other areas, ancient Syria and Palestine were never the home of a great civilization as were Egypt and Mesopotamia. As a result it lacked the prosperity to create large numbers of works of art.

The Amorites

Indeed the earliest pictorial evidence for the dress of the inhabitants of Syria-Palestine comes from a tomb at Beni Hasan in Egypt dating to about 1900 BC. This shows a caravan of 'Aamu', conventionally translated simply as 'Asiatics' but obviously, at this period, representing the Amorites as known from other sources. They are shown leading donkeys which the inscription tells us are carrying black eye paint, a substance used by the ancient Egyptians both as a cosmetic and as a preventative against eye infections. The men wear either knee-length kilts (figure 51) or knee-length garments which partly cover the chest and go over one shoulder, either right or left (figure 52). Both the kilts and the longer garments can have fringes along the bottom. The women (figure 53) wear longer calf-length dresses passing over the left shoulder and with a higher cut than those of the men fitting more tightly under the armpit. These garments were probably fastened at the shoulder by some sort of clasp or dress pin. The garments of both men and women are made of wool and have multicoloured geometrical designs.

Footwear consists of open sandals made from strips of leather for the men and shoes or slippers of a solid material for the women. The men wear their hair cut fairly short at the back and have short pointed beards. The women have long hair which falls naturally down their backs and over their shoulders held in place by a head band.

The figures in this scene probably come close in appearance to the way Abraham and the patriarchal tribes would have looked, certainly not primitive or in any way backward, but lacking the sophisticated polish to which the people of the Egyptian and Mesopotamian civilizations were by now accustomed.

51 A figure from the group of Asiatics shown in the tomb at Beni Hasan in Egypt; he is wearing a short kilt

The Canaanites

The Canaanites gradually infiltrated the area from the north and their culture absorbed and submerged that of the less refined Amorites. However the two peoples continued to live alongside each other; in general the Amorites followed a rural life in the hills whilst the Canaanites renewed an urban existence in the plains.

The earliest depictions of the Canaanite settlers in the Holy Land likewise come from scenes painted in ancient Egyptian tombs, this time dating to the eighteenth dynasty and located in the cliffs at Thebes in Upper Egypt. Some twenty one tombs preserve scenes depicting foreigners presenting tribute to pharaoh. Included amongst these are the Canaanite chieftains of Syria-Palestine and their followers. They are shown wearing a variety of garments.

The simple kilt, already seen on the Amorites, continues in use though in this period it is often draped so as to hang in a point at the front and the seams are often decorated with borders done in blue and red (figure 54). The kilt continues to be worn for many centuries to come especially by the lower echelons of society and, probably for practical reasons, by soldiers.

52   A figure from the same scene in a long cloak

53   One of the women from the ▶ Beni Hasan scene

54   A Canaanite as depicted in a later Egyptian tomb wearing a kilt

Up to the end of the reign of Amenophis II of Egypt (1413 BC) another common dress comprises a long-sleeved, calf-length tunic usually with a V-neck and often with groups of tassels along the hem (figure 55). As with the kilts of this period the tunics usually have seams decorated with bands done in blue and red thread providing a gay contrast with the plain white of the material.

In later depictions (Amenophis III onwards) this same tunic is seen worn but embellished with a long narrow band of cloth, decorated on its edges, wrapped around the upper part of the tunic's skirt (figure 56). Another garment (figure 57) introduced at about the same time and continuing in use at least until the twentieth dynasty (about 1100 BC) ie for three centuries appears to have been draped around the body in a series of folds. This was worn in conjunction with a cape of similar material worn loosely over the shoulders. The materials from which these garments were made were often elaborately patterned with spots or more complicated geometric designs.

The women accompanying the Canaanite chieftains and offering bearers wear either a calf- or ankle-length dress characteristically flounced from the waist downwards, often with three flounces (figure 58). In most instances it appears to have had short sleeves though in several cases a simple cape is worn over the shoulders thus obscuring the sleeves. The women's dresses appear to have been made from plain white material. Where they occur children are shown either naked or wearing a miniature version of one of the adult garments.

Both men and women are shown barefoot in these scenes, presumably out of courtesy because they are within the palace or entering the presence of pharaoh. The men invariably have short, pointed beards though their hair is worn either closely cropped or quite thick and shoulder length; in the latter case it was held in place by a head band. Women have long hair pulled back behind their ears and hanging freely down the back.

Evidence from Syria-Palestine itself is much sparser but generally speaking confirms the picture gleaned from the Egyptian tomb scenes. For example a stela from Ugarit (Ras Shamra) depicting the weather god Baal shows him bare chested and wearing a short kilt with decorative horizontal bands.

The simple long tunic is found on a gilded statue of a deity wearing a conical head-dress. The later Canaanite garment which was wrapped around the body is reflected on a bronze inlay plaque of about 1450 BC (figure 59). Here the garment is shown more tightly wound than in the Egyptian tomb paintings. In addition the cape appears to be much bulkier and is perhaps to be interpreted as a skin; note the leg-like projection over the right shoulder. A fringed or tasselled sash or scarf hangs down between the cape and robe though this is perhaps the end of the piece of cloth which makes up the garment itself.

Similar clothes to those seen in the Egyptian tomb scenes, both men's and women's, are also found amongst the representational designs carved on ivories discovered in the palace at Megiddo. Although many of the

55

56

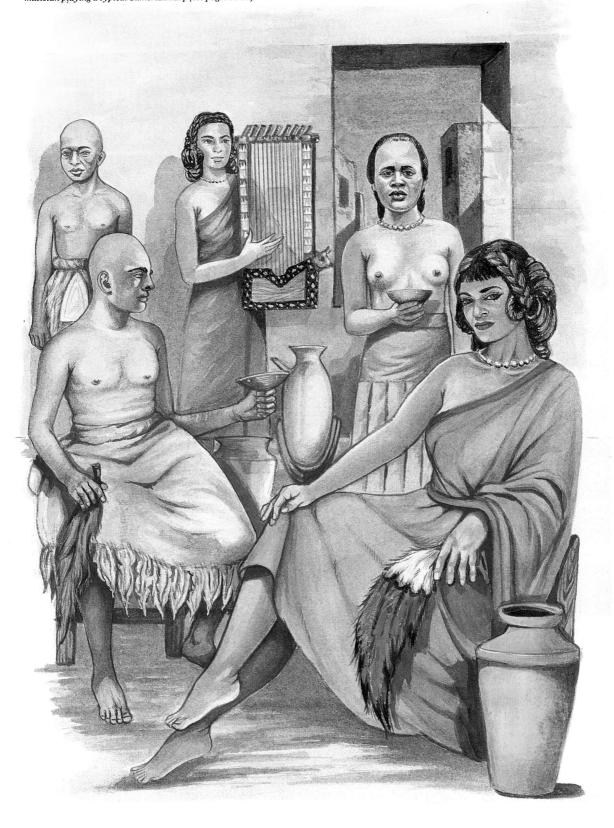

PLATE 1 *A Sumerian banquet showing a man and his wife being served by male and female attendants and entertained by a musician playing a typical Sumerian harp (see pages 11-15)*

PLATE 2 Divine figures and a king taken from the wall paintings in the palace at Mari showing several Old Babylonian garments which were in current use (see pages 27-29)

PLATE 3 *Amorite nomads amidst their semi-desert surroundings (see page 30)*

PLATE 4 Canaanites en route to Egypt laden with tribute for presentation to pharaoh (see pages 31-34)

PLATE 5 A ninth century Aramean king and a king of Damascus standing before a thirteenth century rock relief showing a Hittite king protected by a warrior god (see pages 35-42)

PLATE 6 Israelite prisoners guarded by an Assyrian spearman
following a successful seige against one of their cities (see pages
45-47, 52-53)

PLATE 7 Assurbanipal and his queen celebrating a military victory in a palace garden; the head of a vanquished king hangs from a branch (see pages 48–51, 54)

PLATE 8 *A Persian king with a member of the Susian guard and a Median spearman (see pages 61-63)*

Megiddo ivories are clearly influenced by Egyptian art they remain distinctly Canaanite in detail.

A style of dress worn commonly by figures on Syrian-style seals and most clearly illustrated on a bronze figure of a prince consists of a knee length dress with thick rolled edges and a fringed border which ties around the waist. Although this comes up the back and passes over the shoulders it leaves the chest bare. A tall felt cap often accompanies such fashion (figure 60).

57

55   The same dressed in a long V-neck tunic

56   Canaanite from a slightly later tomb in a so-called 'wound' tunic

57   The same garment worn in conjunction with a cape of similar material

58   Canaanite woman in a flounced dress

59   Canaanite as depicted on a native bronze plaque of c 1450 BC

60   Typically Syrian conical felt hat

58

59

60

A similar but longer, calf-length, garment with thick rolled edges is found on a bronze figurine from Ugarit (figure 61), often unnecessarily described as a goddess. Her dress is not clearly draped but appears to come up the back onto the shoulders where it is held in place by a cord across the front of her neck. Apart from the rolled edge the garment has a fringed border down the centre front and the cloth is decorated with a diamond pattern.

Simpler but more elegant and flowing robes are seen on an ivory figure of a lady from Megiddo (figure 62) and some idea of the elaborate plaiting of ladies' hair at this period can be gained from figure 63.

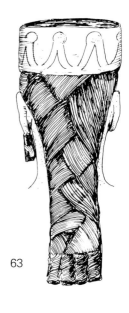

63

61   62

61   Garment with thick rolled edges as exemplified on a bronze figure from Ugarit

62   Canaanite lady in flowing robes

63   Elaborately plaited hair as depicted on an ivory figurine of a woman from Megiddo

5 Hittites and Arameans

Hittite empire   1500-1200 BC
Neo-Hittites
   and Arameans   1100- 700 BC

64   Warrior or weather god in typical Hittite infantry man's dress as shown on the Royal Gate at Bogazkoy

The Hittite capital was at Bogazkoy in central Anatolia, near the modern Turkish village of Hattusas. The greatest period of the Hittite empire was about 1400-1200 BC beginning with king Suppiluliuma who defeated the Mitannians of north Syria and campaigned down as far as northern Palestine. At about the same time there arose a distinctive Hittite style of art which has no known antecedents in Anatolia and, despite showing borrowings from Egypt which were obviously transmitted and modified under Syrian influence, it nevertheless retains a distinctive originality. It is known to us almost exclusively from relief sculptures used to decorate the palaces of the Hittite kings. These sculptures however lack the narrative composition of Egyptian and Assyrian reliefs and deal with purely religious subjects. This being so the knowledge which we can derive from them concerning Hittite costume is limited. The Egyptian reliefs tend to be at variance with the Hittite ones though this will be discussed in the companion volume on Egyptian costume and only the Hittite sources are considered here.

Men's dress

One of the most often quoted and illustrated works of Hittite art is the jamb from the so-called 'Royal Gate' at Bogazkoy, the Hittite capital (figure 64). This depicts a figure dressed as a warrior (infantry) wearing a short, mid-thigh length, kilt or loincloth worn in such a fashion that one edge of the material forms a diagonal line across the front of the figure. The cloth is decorated with alternating horizontal stripes of oblique lines and running spirals. It is held up by a broad metal belt. He wears a pointed helmet with ear flaps descending from the rim and a flexible neck guard at the back. It is surmounted by a crest which droops down the back, pig-tail like, and is decorated with bull's horns in raised relief. The warrior has no protection on his chest, arms, legs or feet. His weapons comprise a characteristic short sword curved at the end and with a pommel in the shape of an inverted crescent as well as a battle axe though the latter is similar to axes found on depictions of weather gods and may not necessarily be a military weapon.

Art historians have debated whether this figure represents a king, a deity or a simple warrior. That it is the king seems unlikely as he is otherwise exclusively depicted wearing the priestly garb described below. A god would seem likely in view of the bull's horns on the helmet.

Be that as it may the dress in general must reflect that of the times as the same short kilt is found on at least two other figures.

The king is always represented dressed as a priest in keeping with the religious tenor of Hittite art (figure 65). He wears a long, ankle-length tunic with a shawl like mantle draped about the arms and shoulders such that a long flap is left hanging down the front of the body. The head is covered with a close fitting skull cap with a thickened band at the rim. On his feet are shoes or some sort of moccasin with pointed up-turned footwear characteristic of the Hittite imperial period and earlier; for example pottery vessels in the shape of boots with up-turned toes have been found dating to the nineteenth century BC. As a symbol of his position the king carries the curved priestly staff.

At a site called Yazilikaya, a short distance north east of Bogazkoy, there is an open air sanctuary which preserves an important set of reliefs showing a procession of the gods and includes every deity of the official pantheon distinguished by the hieroglyphic symbol used to write his or her name.

The gods on these reliefs for the most part wear a short, belted tunic or short kilts, fluted conical head-dresses with a thickened, possibly rolled, rim and upturned shoes. These are more clearly seen on a relief from the lion gate at Malataya (figure 66) which is dated by some scholars to the post

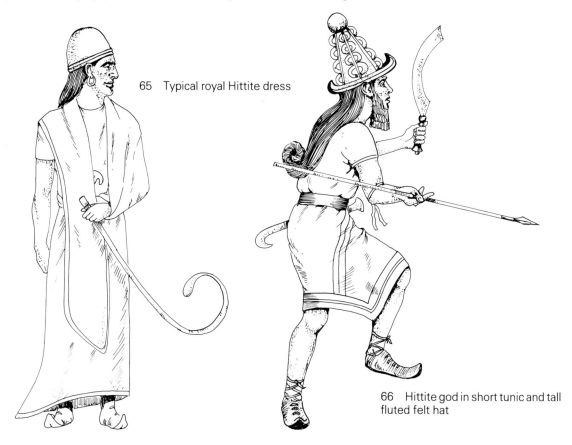

65 Typical royal Hittite dress

66 Hittite god in short tunic and tall fluted felt hat

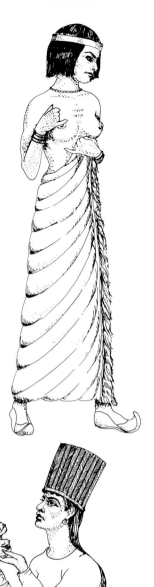

imperial period. Nevertheless it retains all the features of imperial Hittite costume. Note that the kilt is worn in the traditional way with the edge of the material running diagonally across the front though it is here draped or cut in such a manner as to produce two curving hems above the knees.

Women's dress

Even fewer depictions of Hittite women are preserved from the imperial period. A relief from Alaça Hüyük shows a queen behind a king approaching the altar of a bull god. Unfortunately the figure of the queen is damaged (figure 67) though she wears a long ankle-length robe draped in a series of close, curved horizontal folds with a fringed edge running down the front. How this was arranged on the shoulders cannot be determined but she appears to hold one end of the garment in her left hand. Her headgear and/or hairstyle is not preserved and on her feet she has the typical upturned shoes.

The goddesses on the Yazilikaya reliefs wear long pleated skirts flaring out at the back and held by a belt with a much looser blouse which drapes across the arms. Upturned shoes are worn. Their head-dresses like those of the gods are fluted but rather than being conical are cylindrical with straight sides and flat tops; in addition they have a pig-tail like streamer hanging down the back (figure 68).

The Neo-Hittite era

The Hittite empire came to an end during the disturbed era of the movements of the Aegean Sea Peoples, the ripples of whose migrations were felt throughout the eastern Mediterranean and Near East. In Anatolia itself the Hittites were replaced by the Phrygians whilst in the south eastern provinces of the Hittite empire (north Syria and Taurus area) Hittite traditions survived for at least five further centuries. Sculptured relief was included amongst these survivals though it appears primitive indeed compared to Assyrian reliefs of the same period.

67 Hittite queen; based on a relief from Alaça Hüyük

68 Hittite goddess from the reliefs at Yazilikaya

Middle Neo-Hittite c 900-750 BC

The art of the middle neo-Hittite period is very much a hybrid tradition retaining many classical Hittite features whilst at the same time incorporating new influences from the artistic canons of surrounding cultures. Our knowledge is derived largely from sculptures from Zincirli and Carchemish.

The short kilt seen on the warrior from the Bogazkoy gate (page 35) remains in use by warriors and the equally warlike weather gods. A warrior from Carchemish wears a helmet very similar to that on the Bogazkoy warrior with a crest on top and bull's horns projecting from the front of the helmet. The ear flaps have been extended however to form a broad chin-guard or strap (figure 69).

Some figures wear a narrow brimmed hat with the appearance of a truncated cone surmounted by a ball. On the Zincirli reliefs the upturned Hittite shoes are retained though it is possible that these were not the height of fashion by the ninth century BC (figure 70).

The majority of the male figures on the ninth-eighth century reliefs from Zincirli and Carchemish, however, characteristically wear a long tunic. This ends slightly above the ankles, has short sleeves and is shaped at the waist by a broad metal belt with rounded edges. Even the king of Carchemish is shown wearing this same unpretentious dress (figure 71). On one example from Zincirli a tassel hangs from the belt (figure 72) though this was not common. The old-fashioned upturned shoes are replaced on these figures by delicately worked open sandals.

New fashions in male coiffure also arise at this period. The hair itself is curled then rolled into a turned up knot at the nape of the neck (figure 71). Beards are normally wedge-shaped, cut straight across the bottom, though the top lip is always left clean shaven. Soldiers and servants are often clean shaven.

Women's dress

A new feature of the neo-Hittite period is a woman's ankle-length mantle or shawl which comes up the back and runs up over the head onto the forehead all but covering the face. At the front the material is cut away to expose the face and allow some movement of the arms. Underneath they wear a simple tunic similar to the men's, held in at the waist by a belt made up of several parallel strands of cord though doubtless royal ladies would have had belts decorated with precious metals (figure 73).

The Late Neo-Hittite Period

With time, increasing pressure of foreign influences, especially Assyrian and Aramean, Hittite features were stifled. Aramean and Assyrian treatment of hair curls became the norm though how much this was the fashion of the times rather than artistic convention is difficult to determine.

69   Neo-Hittite spearman's helmet

70   Neo-Hittite warrior

71   The most characteristic neo-
Hittite garment was a long tunic as
worn here by the king of Carchemish

72   Neo-Hittite tunic with a tassel
from the belt

73   A new feature of neo-Hittite
women's dress was the shawl
which came up over the head

Men's dress

A relief from Carchemish shows a king and his son both dressed in short-sleeved ankle-length tunics differing from those of the earlier period by having a series of small vertical pleats down the back such as we have already seen on the *kudurru* of Marduk-apla-iddina (page 26, figure 45). The prince's tunic is held by a belt which is decorated at the terminals and from which a long tassel hangs. The king wears a loosely draped over garment with a herringbone border (figure 74).

Another important source for this period is a series of funerary stelae from Maras. These show the men wearing the same simple tunic as in middle neo-Hittite times with broad metal belts. However, the Maras figures have a wide apron which is fringed at the bottom. It has been suggested that this is an Aramean custom though in any event it is doubtless derived from the earlier fashion of having a single tassel hanging from the belt (figure 75).

Another stela (figure 76) showing a boy standing in his mother's lap gives an example of this same simple tunic adorned by the addition of a fringe or vertical pleats along the bottom edge and an embroidered collar. He also has equally elegant sandals.

75

74

76

40

Women's dress

The ladies of the late neo-Hittite period wore tunics similar to those of the men held in at the waist by multi-strand belts as in the middle neo-Hittite period. These were either plain (figure 76) or had their lower skirts pleated or gathered into vertical folds (figure 77). The shawl coming up onto the head which we saw introduced earlier (figure 73) continues in use though it now often has a knotted border and appears much less voluminous (figure 76 and 77). It is quite clear from these that it is a separate garment.

The Arameans

The Arameans make their first appearance in history during the latter half of the second millennium as bands of Semitic nomads migrating from their home in the Arabian desert into Babylonia and northern Syria. By the eleventh century BC an Aramean was king of Babylon after which there was a steady influx of Arameans into Babylonia. In a similar fashion they infiltrated northern Syria and by the eighth-seventh centuries BC the major political (and therefore the major economic and cultural) cities were under their domination.

Because of their nomadic origins and because they were inhabiting an area which had received constant influence, direct or indirect, from Egypt (via Syria), Hittites, Mitannians and Assyrians and one which was still recovering from the upheavals caused by the migrations of the Sea Peoples the art of the Aramean rulers of north Syria was very hybrid. Indeed it is wrong and of little value to name it after a particular people and although we have above discussed a neo-Hittite tradition this is equally misleading and is really no more than an accumulation of works which show imperial Hittite traits, in a more or less bastardized form, or a logical development of these. In this section therefore we will deal with the remaining pieces as Aramean, for the nomads must have contributed something from their own culture to the art of the area, but with the warning that this may well not have the ethnic implications that the modern reader might infer.

77

74   A king and his son both wearing long tunics with pleats at the back; from Carchemish

75   Man with wide apron at the front

76   Boy with his mother; both costumes show the developing style of the period

77   Woman wearing long tunic with pleated skirt

Men's dress

One of the earliest so-called Aramean pieces is a relief from Zincirli of king Kilamuwa with his son (figure 78). They both wear a spirally wound garment forming a cape over the shoulders and held at the waist by a belt. It is very similar to the costume worn by the Canaanites of a few centuries earlier (figure 57). Both wear shoes or sandals with filled in heels. The prince is clean shaven and the king has the wedge-shaped beard but a clean shaven top lip; both have curled hair gathered into a turned up knot at the back. In respect of coiffure therefore they follow the neo-Hittite norm. Indeed only the head-dress of the king is at all novel and it has been suggested that this rounded turban-like headgear surmounted by a point is original to the Arameans.

A garment similarly draped but with more and much more closely spaced diagonal folds is found on a royal figure from Sakcegozu of about 730 BC (figure 79). The edges of the material are fringed or tasselled and one corner of the garment passes over the right shoulder and is held in the left hand. Below the bottom fringed border is a second plain hem the back of which appears to have vertical pleats. These surely cannot be part of the same garment and presumably the figure wears a back-pleated tunic as we have already encountered above (page 26) beneath the spirally wound cloak. Footwear consists of open sandals with solid heel pieces. The hair, which is held in place by a decorative band, is neo-Hittite in style apart from the long curl in front of the ear which is possibly a specifically Aramean trait.

A stela of king Barrelin from Zincirli is shown with the supposed Aramean head-dress and curl but he is otherwise dressed in a simple tunic, fringed with loops of thread along the bottom hem, with a similarly fringed cape thrown over his shoulders. His secretary is shown in an even plainer long tunic and is clean shaven.

Women's dress

A princess on a funerary stela from Zincirli wears a typical neo-Hittite tunic with pleated skirt (figure 80) and fringed hem. Above her curled hair is an Aramean head-piece adorned on its rim with a band decorated with six-leaf rosettes which also trails ribbon-like from the back of the hat. On her breast the lady wears a Phrygian fibula, a popular accessory in the eighth century.

78   An Aramean king

79   A more elaborate version of the
long tunic with diagonal folds

80   A princess from Zincirli in a
typical pleated skirt with fringed hem

78

79

80

6 Israelites and Phoenicians

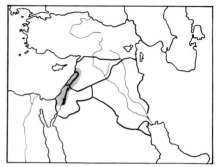

Israelites and Phoenicians
1100-500 BC

Evidence for the costume of the inhabitants of the Holy Land in later Old Testament times is very sparse and somewhat conflicting. Possibly because of this it is often stated that the Biblical peoples dressed in the fashion of modern Arab bedouin. This suggestion however is unfounded though there may have been some superficial similarities between the ancient garments, especially the simpler ones, and those of the bedouin.

Evidence from the Bible

The Bible mentions and in some instances describes the clothes of the period. The familiar wrap-around kilt reaching to the mid thighs ('*ezor*) seems to have been confined to military personnel. They were made of linen or leather and held in place by a waistband (*hagorah*) secured by tying the ends, which were often elaborately decorated together. The upper body was covered with a simple T-shaped shirt.

Shirts or tunics (*kuttonet*, Greek *chiton*) appear to have been the normal dress and most people would have possessed one. Woven from either linen or wool they could be knee-length or ankle-length and could have long sleeves, short sleeves or no sleeves.

For warmth a cloak (*simlah*) was worn as an over-garment and these came in a variety of materials and styles. The crudest ones were made from hides whilst the finely woven wool or linen examples achieved a relatively close fit. They were open down the front and had decorated borders along the edges. Otherwise a variety of cuts are mentioned ranging from simple shawl-like squares, capes with slits in the sides for the arms to pass through up to cloaks with short sleeves.

The dress normally worn by priests consisted of a simple loincloth covering the hips and thighs over which was a long embroidered linen tunic with sleeves. Accessories included a belt and a turban but not sandals as they were not allowed to be worn in temples. Priests were forbidden to wear clothes made from wool. The vestments of the high priest are described in Exodus chapter 28 and various reconstructions of these have been attempted, some more fanciful than others.

Women's dress must have been similar to men's as they normally wore a *kuttonet* and a *simlah*. However, whilst the men in most instances wore the tunic next to the skin women had fine underwear (*sadin*). There were presumably other noticeable differences as it was forbidden for men to

81

81   Israelite presenting tribute to the Assyrian king

82   Israelite prisoner in a simple, plain tunic

83   Israelite archer captured during the siege of Lachish

44

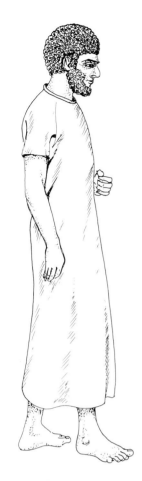

82

83

wear women's clothes and vice versa. Possibly the women would have used finer or more highly decorated materials and certainly ladies of rank wore veils or had long trains.

The normal custom amongst the Israelites was for both sexes to have long hair and baldness was disliked. It was not until New Testament times that it was shameful for men to have long hair. Women frequently braided or plaited their hair.

Depictions of Israelites and their neighbours

The major depictions of Israelites occur on Assyrian sculptures of the ninth and eighth centuries. Shalmaneser's Black Obelisk (about 825 BC) shows the Assyrian king receiving the tribute of Jehu of Israel. The Israelite tribute bearers (figure 81) are dressed in tunics with a fringed hem stopping above the ankle over which is worn a cloak open down the front and also with a fringed border. It has been suggested that this is a representation of the Hebrew *me'il* though in quite what way these differed from the *simlah* is uncertain. It is immediately apparent that these garments have more in common with the contemporary neo-Hittite and Aramean fashions than with the Canaanite costume of the late bronze age. The use of Hittite up-turned shoes by the Israelites in this scene is hard to explain. The men have traditional Canaanite pointed beards but have shaved upper lips in neo-Hittite fashion. They wear a pointed cap which flops over at the end, perhaps a kind of turban or *keffiyeh*.

The later reliefs of Sennacherib recording the siege of Lachish (701 BC) shows Israelite captives being led out of the city. At the head of the procession are men with close cut hair and beards wearing a simple tunic of plain material (figure 82). This probably represents the basic *kuttonet* and on these examples it extends more than half way down the lower leg but stops above the ankle and has short sleeves which cover about two thirds of the upper arm. No decoration of any sort is indicated though it is known that on finer examples the bottom edge and often the collar had borders of finely woven and brightly coloured material or were intricately embroidered.

Towards the rear of the file of captives are other men who, to judge by their dress, are captive soldiers, perhaps archers (figure 83). They wear a short mid-thigh length wrap-round skirt over which is a short tunic with short sleeves, very similar in appearance to a modern T-shirt. A broad, four-stranded belt secures both the tunic and the skirt about the waist. They have a piece of cloth wrapped turban-like about their heads with the fringed end dangling over one ear to the shoulder.

A relief of the Assyrian king Tiglathpileser III (about 730 BC) shows prisoners captured at a town south of Damascus dressed in exactly the same fashion as the Israelites on the Black Obelisk with the exception of their headgear which lacks the droop at the end.

An ivory plaque from Arslan Tash of slightly earlier date depicts a ruler of Damascus similarly dressed but, not inappropriately, with a more refined cut to his robes (figure 84). His shoulder length hair hangs naturally, without any indication of elaborate curling, held back by a thin headband or fillet; his long beard comes to a rounded point. He wears open sandals with a strap across the instep and solid heel pieces.

A statue of an Ammonite ruler displays a mixture of styles (figure 85). The basic garment consists of a long tunic with short sleeves, somewhat unusual in being pleated all over. The tassel hanging from a hidden belt echoes neo-Hittite or Aramean practice whilst later Canaanite traditions are evident in the strip of cloth which is wound bandolier like round his upper body. The ends of this are knotted and frayed, one end thrown over the right shoulder.

84   The king of Damascus in finely cut robes

◀ 85   Ammonite figure wearing a peculiar mixture of fashions

46

Israelite women

The captives on the siege of Lachish reliefs mentioned above include several women all of whom are dressed alike (figure 86). Their very simple tunics are identical to those of the men as already described (figure 82) above. In addition they wear a piece of cloth drawn up over their heads but without the borders found on Aramean examples.

The Phoenicians

After the disruptions caused by the Sea Peoples in the twelfth century the inland cities of Syria, as we have seen, continued Hittite traditions and drew largely on the art of Assyria for new inspiration. The inhabitants of the coastal cities of Syria and northern Palestine, the Phoenicians, however turned towards Egypt. The most characteristic feature of Phoenician art during the period under consideration is the frequent use of typical Egyptian motifs but executed and used in a way such that it is obvious that the artists had no knowledge of their true context or significance. This is seen to best advantage on the many thousands of carved ivory furniture inlays which have been discovered in Syria and, especially, at Nimrud in northern Iraq (Assyria). Much work remains to be done on the stylistic analysis of these ivories. Obviously the figures wearing bungled versions of Egyptian costumes are to be regarded as instances of fossilized motifs surviving amongst the repertoire of designs used by the Phoenician craftsmen. Many other figures wear costumes which reflect those found on neo-Hittite sculptures both from southern Anatolia and from sites in northern Syria such as Tell Halaf.

Evidence from other sources suggests that the Phoenicians probably continued their indigenous Canaanite traditions, for a time at least. These were gradually modified with elements from the dress of their more immediate neighbours.

Certainly they maintained the reputation for wearing brightly coloured clothes and Homer refers to the polychrome garments of the inhabitants of Sidon. Indeed textile dyeing was a major Phoenician industry and they held a monopoly in it, at least throughout the eastern world. Tyre and Sidon were the two most important centres. Species of the *Murex* shellfish were used, which, when dead and beginning to putrefy secreted a yellowish liquid. It was extracted by breaking the shells off and leaving the exposed fish to rot in vats from which the liquid could be collected. The dye produced a range of shades from rose-pink to dark violet depending on the strength used and the degree of exposure to sunlight. For the darker tones strong solutions and long exposure were needed. Vast heaps containing the remains of many millions of shells have been found near both Sidon and Tyre and there is archaeological evidence for this industry from many other sites.

In later times the Phoenicians fell under increasing Greek influence and their dress followed Hellenistic fashions.

86   Israelite woman captured at Lachish

7   The Assyrians

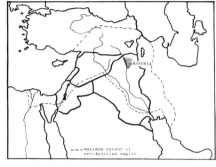

Neo-Assyria   1100-600 BC

The Assyrian empire rose out of very humble beginnings. In the early second millennium its capital city Assur was a small city state which derived its prosperity from trading tin and textiles to southern Anatolia, especially the merchant colony at Kanish. By 1350 it was the capital of an expanding state roughly occupying the triangle of land between Assur, Nineveh and Arbil. From the ninth century until the fall of Nineveh in 612 BC the Assyrians ruled a mighty empire which, at its height, reached as far as Egypt.

The Assyrian kings of the ninth to seventh centuries erected monumental palaces in various cities which were decorated with raised relief sculptures carved in stone. These provide us with a major and invaluable source of pictorial evidence about Assyrian costume. They arose out of a tradition of wall painting and originally they would have been painted in bright colours but today only traces of paint remain; hints of black on the beards and red on the sandal straps for instance.

Men's costume

The King

The Assyrian kings are shown dressed in a variety of garments. The most elaborate outfit consists of a long, ankle-length, tunic with short sleeves and a rounded neck at the front. This is very much like an elongated modern T-shirt and was probably only made up from two pieces of material with two side seams and two shoulder seams. Over this is worn a large shawl, probably made from a square piece of material which is draped over the abdomen and legs helter-skelter wise from the waist. The shoulders and upper body were covered with a smaller probably semi-circular shawl. The shawls were held in place by a braided waist band. This costume is seen to best advantage on a statue of king Assurnasirpal II from Nimrud (figure 87). It was in use throughout the neo-Assyrian period and Esarhaddon is seen wearing it on a stela which he had set up in Zincirli (figure 88). There is evidence to suggest that this combination was worn particularly at religious ceremonies. Long shawls otherwise are confined to use by queens, other important ladies and the so-called genies, figures which represent demi-gods or beneficent demons. They are usually winged, sometimes in the form of griffons and are shown in various symbolic scenes of purely ritual significance. Sometimes only the larger

87   The Assyrian king Assurnasirpal II

48

square shawl is used to cover both lower and upper body in which cases it is of course draped in a different manner.

Another item which also appears to have been solely for royal use is a short square back-apron over the buttocks (figure 89). It very often has knotted and tasselled edges with longer tassels suspended from the corners on long cords. It is worn exclusively with the ankle-length tunic secured by a broad belt. It should not be confused with similar aprons worn by genies which always have rounded corners. Rarely, kings are shown wearing a longer, almost ankle-length, back-apron stopping just above the bottom of the tunic; the longer aprons always have rounded corners.

When practicality demanded it the king wore a shorter, almost knee-length, tunic also with short sleeves. In figure 90 it is worn in conjunction with a wrap-around skirt or apron which is shorter at the front than at the back and is made from elaborate material decorated with royal rosettes. The wide belt is equally ornate.

88   Esarhaddon, king of Assyria, in full court dress

89   The Assyrian king wearing a short square back apron

90   Assurbanipal in elaborate hunting tunic with diagonal hem

91   A eunuch dressed for court

Officials and servants

It is not necessary here to separate rigorously the various minor royalty, officials, attendants and servants who are shown in the company of the king. Generally speaking the higher the social or official position of a person the more elaborate was his dress. Members of the royal family and the highest officials wore dress very similar to that of the king himself but, obviously, in less luxurious materials. Other officials are most frequently shown in ankle-length tunics with a drape over their upper bodies only (figure 91). This is usually described as being a short fringed shawl worn over a similarly fringed belt or girdle. Other depictions give the impression of having a fringed girdle with a sash, again of fringed material, tucked underneath it. In reality these probably represent one and the same fashion which may in fact have been a single piece of fringed material which was wrapped around the waist then passed under one arm and diagonally across the chest, thrown over the opposite shoulder and tucked in beneath the girdle. Again knee-length tunics were substituted when hunting or riding. Also various intermediate lengths can be exemplified, lower calf being the most common of these.

The king's personal attendants, both men and eunuchs (it is generally assumed that those figures which are shown without beards are eunuchs), wear tunics variously with or without the 'belt and sash' (figure 92). In the seventh century a difference arises in that whilst the eunuchs continue to wear tunics in imitation of court dress, the men sport knee-length kilts, often with a fringed border dangling down between the knees (figure 93). This feature of the kilt first comes into vogue during the reign of Tiglathpileser III (744-727) and is never found in the ninth century.

Scribes can often be recognized by the clay tablets, writing boards or scrolls which they carry. They usually wear long tunics on the earlier reliefs but from the reign of Sennacherib (704-681) onwards more often have short tunics.

Musicians are shown in long tunics with fringed belts and sashes to support their instruments (figure 94) as well as in much plainer tunics with simple cord belts. Several examples are found in which the hem is higher at the front than at the back (figure 95).

Ordinary workers had either plain short tunics, obviously of coarser material, secured by belts or wore kilts with a bare torso (figue 96).

◄ 92   A royal attendant

93   Assyrian man in knee-length kilt
with pendent fringed border

94   Musician in long tunic

95   A musician in a tunic with
diagonal hem

96   The royal dog keeper wearing a
kilt

Military costume

In the earlier periods the Assyrian kings raised armies as and when needed but from the eighth century at least there is evidence to suggest that a regular 'standing' army was maintained. The army can be divided into officers, cavalry including chariotry, and infantry. From the point of view of costume however it is more convenient to divide the combined cavalry, chariotry and infantry into Assyrian regulars, auxilliary recruits and provincial contingents.

The officers, depending on situation, can be found in anything from full court dress to the simple archer's kilt. They are usually distinguishable by carrying a mace symbolic of their power and authority though in scenes depicting the fiercer moments of battle even this is often omitted.

Of the regular Assyrian troops archers are the commonest and they most usually wear a short kilt with a thin sash across their chest to support their quivers. Normally they are armed only with bows but could also carry swords or daggers (figure 97). The next most important element were the spearmen who again are normally shown in short kilts (figure 98). As well as a long spear they invariably carry shields and quite frequently also swords or daggers. Only under kings Tiglathpileser III and Sennacherib are slingmen found. For the most part the cavalry comprised mounted archers or mounted spearmen.

Heavy armour was known to the Assyrians and indeed fragments of iron scale armour, which was doubtless sewn onto a leather or stout cloth backing, have been found in excavations. The reliefs show two usages. A short waist length armoured shirt is worn over a knee length tunic by some cavalry men. Infantry men on the other hand had a full length armoured suit with a separate neck and cheek guard rather like the lower part of a balaclava helmet in appearance (figure 99).

The auxilliary recruits represent obvious foreign elements within the Assyrian army though they seem to have become progressively more Assyrianized with time. Auxilliaries are only rarely encountered in the ninth century reliefs but are commonly shown from the reign of Tiglathpileser III onwards. Several categories of auxilliary archers can be discerned though in general they all wore headbands and short kilts often decorated with geometric patterns. It has been suggested that their origins should be sought amongst the Arameans.

The auxilliary spearmen are easily recognized by their crested helmets (page 58) and they invariably wear short tunics rather than kilts (figure 100). They are further distinguished by having two straps which cross behind a roundel on their chest and go over the shoulders. Standard weapons were spear, circular shield and sword.

The provincial troops are often attired in their native dress though it is possible that Assyrian 'uniforms' were on occasions issued to them.

97   A seventh century Assyrian archer

52

98

100

98 A seventh century Assyrian
spearman

99 A suit of scale armour

100 Auxilliary spearman in a typical
crested helmet

99

Religious costumes

Mention has already been made of various semi-divine figures, conventionally referred to as genies, and these are found in a variety of garbs including the long tunic with long shawl as worn by the king (figures 87 and 88). Most usual though is a short tunic with a long, ankle-length back apron meeting at the front across the waist but cut away in a sweeping curve at either side to leave the front open (figure 101). Shorter aprons are worn but these again are rounded, never square like the ones worn by the king.

Genies are also shown in short tunics with an over garment consisting of an ankle-length coat with short sleeves. This wraps over itself on the chest and is held by a belt but is left to flare open below the waist (figure 102).

A variety of distinctive 'characters' are also encountered, many of whom were doubtless priests dressed in costumes appropriate to particular ceremonies or festivals. Commonest of these are the fishman (figure 103) and the lion demon (figure 104).

The Queen

There are few depictions of women on the reliefs and most of the ones that do occur are of foreign women taken prisoner on the campaigns. Representations of Assyrian women are very rare and the most famous and best preserved is that of queen Assur-Sharrat, wife of Assurbanipal (figure 105). She is dressed in very similar fashion to the king with a long fringed tunic and single shawl wrapped around lower and upper body. The main difference is that her tunic has sleeves which come about half way down her lower arm rather than the short sleeves normally encountered on men's tunics. Similar fashions are seen on other royal ladies of the period.

Materials

Assyrian tunics were often made out of fine materials and royal ones at least had very elaborate decoration on them including intricately embroidered designs depicting mythological scenes and rosettes sewn on rather like modern sequins. Certain designs were more favoured at particular periods. For example material with a pattern of concentric squares was introduced in the reign of Tiglathpileser III and is particularly frequently encountered then though it is occasionally found later but never earlier. The edges of cloth were often fringed, tasselled or knotted and frayed, occasionally beaded. Most tunics had a border along the bottom edge and round the sleeves. The body of the tunic was often patterned with geometric designs made up from squares, diamonds, rosettes, stars, circles, dots, hexagons, etc, or combinations of these. Royal garments could have panels of very elaborate embroidered decoration on the chest producing the effect of a pectoral.

101

101 Typical dress of the semi-divine genies

102 Genie in a short tunic with 'overcoat'

103 A fish-man

104 A lion-man

105 Queen Assur-sharrat, wife of Assurbanipal; this is one of the rare depictions of Assyrian women

102

104

103

105

Footwear

Under most circumstances the vast majority of people would have gone barefoot. However sandals were by no means uncommon possessions and are frequently shown on the reliefs, worn by both the king and his subjects. There is an apparent subtle change in the style of sandals during the neo-Assyrian period. In the ninth century the heel pieces are quite long and extend all the way to the base of the little toe; during the reign of Tiglathpileser III they come about half way along the foot whilst under Sargon II and later kings they cover the heel only.

Sandals were made up of a sole, a heel piece, a strap across the big toe and were secured across the instep either by laces which passed through holes in the heel pieces or by thongs passing through rings or hoops attached separately to the heel pieces. (figure 106a and b).

What have been described variously as shoes or moccasins are more rarely found and these were probably a kind of slipper made from a fairly soft material or thin leather (figure 107a). More elaborate, 'lace-up' shoes are also documented (figure 107b and c).

From the reign of Sargon II (721-705) boots were introduced, especially for military personnel, extending to either mid-calf or knee length. They must have had laces down the front as the depictions suggest and the knee length examples seem to have been 'bandaged' around the upper leg. The area of leg between boot top and tunic bottom is always shown with criss-cross hatching and it is normally assumed from this that some sort of woven or netted stocking was worn in conjunction with the boots (figure 108a and b).

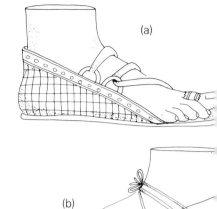

106   Examples of Assyrian sandals

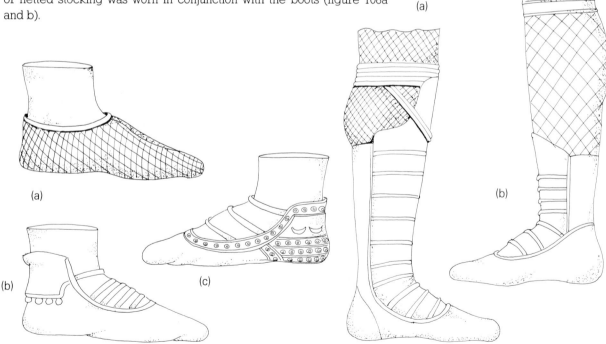

107   Examples of Assyrian shoes

108   Examples of Assyrian boots

Headgear

On all official occasions the king wore a fez-like head-dress, hardly a crown, with a rounded projection on top and two ribbons pendent from the back. This is often referred to as a *polos* in the literature. The earliest Assyrian king to be shown wearing this head-dress is Tukulti-Ninurta I (1244-1208). An origin in Babylonia has been suggested as Kassites are shown wearing it in the fourteenth century. In the ninth century the royal *polos* has a band around the base with a rosette placed centre front. With Tiglathpileser III two additional bands of decoration are sometimes indicated near the top and from his reign onwards the *polos* becomes gradually taller and more ornate. On some of Sargon II's reliefs even the cone on top has bands of decoration and is adorned with rosettes, the traditional symbol of royalty (figure 109a, b and c).

When hunting the king wore a simple fillet, taller at the front than at the back (figure 109d). In religious scenes he is normally depicted bare-headed.

Officials are commonly shown bare-headed but occasionally wear head bands.

(a)

(b)

(c)

(d)

109　Varieties of royal head-dress

All Assyrian soldiers in the ninth century were equipped with pointed helmets for battle as were most troops in succeeding centuries. In the seventh century some helmets had ear flaps (figure 110a and b).

Auxilliary spearmen wore crested helmets. From the reign of Tiglathpileser III the crests curved forwards either with or without feathers and this gradually became the standard type (figure 110c and d), though many variant forms can also be documented (figure 110e and f). Auxilliary archers wore simple headbands.

Priests had very characteristic tall hats, rather like inverted flower vases (figure 111a) though it is possible that these are only to be associated with a specific type of musician priest. The genies wear various crowns all of which are shown with bull's horns in relief, a symbol of their divinity (figure 111b and c).

Assur-sharrat wears a castellated fillet probably set with jewels and Naqia, mother of Esarhaddon, wears a similar crown.

(b)

(a)

(a)

(b)

(c)

110   Military helmets

(d)

(e)

(f)

(c)

111   Religious headgear

58

8 Elamites and Persians

Middle Elamite   500- 330 BC
Achaemenid empire
(Perisans)   1400-1000 BC

The first urban civilization arose in Iran about 2800 BC in the area known in ancient times as Elam, corresponding roughly to the modern region of Khuzistan in south western Iran. It was contemporary with the Sumerian civilization in Mesopotamia and derived much inspiration and influence from that source. The Iranian speaking peoples first entered Iran about 1400 BC spreading from the north east westwards into Azerbaijan and then south to the valleys of the Zagros mountains. The Medes are first mentioned in Assyrian clay tablets in 836 BC and the Persians in 844 BC. The Median capital was located at Ecbatana (modern Hamadan) in central western Iran whilst the Persians occupied Persia (modern Fars) in the south. In alliance with the Babylonians the Medes overthrew the Assyrian empire in 612 BC though it was the Persians who were destined to take over the role of world leaders. The Persian king Cyrus the Great (559-530) united Media and Persia into a single state, defeated king Croesus of Lydia and brought the juvenile neo-Babylonian empire to an end; his troops marched into Babylon unopposed in 539 BC. Darius I (552-486) built on these foundations the greatest near eastern empire ever, usually referred to as the Achaemenid empire, until it too fell to a conquering force, that of Alexander the Great, whose burning of Persepolis in 330 BC effectively signalled the end of the ancient near east.

Elamites and Early Iranians

In the earlier periods Elamite art was largely overshadowed by contemporary Mesopotamian, Sumerian and Akkadian, conventions. As a result all the depictions of dress from early Elam can be paralleled in Mesopotamia. Two statues from Elam, contemporary with the Early Dynastic period in Sumer, exemplify this. One of them represents a man wearing a shaggy kilt with a piece drawn over the left shoulder, the other a woman wearing a shaggy cloak which is brought over both shoulders and covers the arms. Both of these garments are identical to ones found on Mesopotamian sculptures. From the end of the third millennium (twenty first century) there is a rock relief which shows a king of one of the mountain tribes wearing a short kilt like that worn by Naram-Sin on his victory stela (figure 29) standing before a goddess in the familiar flounced dress.

A distinctive native style emerges in the middle-Elamite period during the latter half of the second millennium. The finest representation is a bronze statue of Queen Napirasu (figure 112), wife of King Untashgal who

112   Queen Napirasu from Susa wearing one of the most elegant garments depicted in the art of the ancient near east

came to the throne about 1275 BC. She wears a short sleeved tunic held in at the waist by a belt; the skirt flares out to produce an elegant and flowing elongated bell shape. The material of the skirt and bodice is decorated with tiny rings and the bottom edge has a border of long wavy fringes. The upper part of the skirt back is covered by a semi-circular apron of fringed or, perhaps more likely, pleated material. Across the waist and running vertically down the centre front is a broad band of decoration done in alternating stripes of zigzag lines and hatching.

Similar but simpler garments are seen on two small figurines from Susa both of whom are shown carrying sacrificial goats. They wear long tunics though the skirts are not as flared and the fringed hems not so wide as on Napirasu's dress (figure 113). The material of the skirts is decorated with dots and the bodices with stars. The men have long tapering beards and wear braided head bands.

A gold bowl from Hasanlu in north western Iran of about the same period (twelfth to eleventh century) is decorated with a crowded and busy scene depicting figures in several different types of dress. There are men in short kilts with tassels hanging from the hems (figure 114) whilst other men wear long tunics with fringed edges or seams running obliquely round their bodies (figure 115) like the later Canaanite garments. The women (figure 116) are shown in a full length robe which covers their entire body. This comprised a single square piece of material with cords at two corners as can be seen from a depiction of a goddess (figure 117) on the same bowl who stands naked on the back of two rams holding her robe behind her in out-stretched arms rather as if drying her back with a bath towel. That this is the same garment as is worn by the women can be intimated from the material which has the same design of vertical stripes of dots. Similar decoration is indicated on the men's kilts and it may possibly represent more a part of the metalworker's repertoire of designs than the weaver's.

113 Man wearing a garment similar to Napirasu's but less elegant

114-117 Figures from the Hasanlu gold bowl

114 Man in a kilt

115 Man in diagonally draped ▶ robes

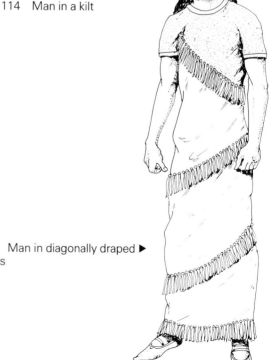

60

116 Woman in long cloak

117   Goddess with a long cloak

Persians

With the Achaemenid empire we encounter a costume which is entirely different from anything we have hitherto come across from the ancient near east. Its essential elements comprised a pair of trousers and a shirt or jacket sufficiently long to be secured around the waist by a belt. However this is not immediately apparent from the sculptures which adorned the buildings of the Achaemenid empire as the Persian kings, the royal family and the high officials favoured a style of dress which followed the traditional near eastern lines of flowing robes.

Often referred to as the 'Robe of Honour' because of its adoption by the king it was arranged in such a way that it fell in a series of ripples at the front and back but with vertical folds falling down the sides giving an illusion of pleating. The arms were draped so as to allow them a maximum degree of movement as a result of which the robe appears to have wide sleeves gathered at the shoulder (figure 118). The materials from which these robes were made could be plain, especially for the lesser members of the

◀ 118   Typical Achaemenid royal dress

61

royal family and the nobles, but the finer examples were decorated very much after the fashion of Assyrian royal tunics. The cloth itself was often coloured and had designs made up from various geometric elements as well as the royal rosette. The edges were often adorned with even more elaborate borders. Some commentators have suggested that trousers were worn beneath the robe. The state head-dress consisted of a castellated fillet or crown with decoration on the band (figure 119) probably set with precious and semi-precious stones. Lace-up shoes for the feet would complete the costume.

The Persian and Susian soldiers of the royal guard, the ten thousand so-called 'Immortals', also wore the robe of honour either with a Persian fluted felt hat (figure 120) or with a Susian braided head band. Those depicted in glazed brick friezes at the palace at Susa wear colourful and highly decorated robes (figure 121) and carry a spear, a bow and a large quiver.

The trousered costume to which we referred above is most frequently met with on depictions of figures who are now generally assumed to be Medes. It comprises a pair of fairly tight fitting trousers, possibly of leather,

119 Castellated crown as worn by king Darius on the Behistun relief

120

121

120 A Persian soldier

121 One of the Susian royal guards

122 A Median soldier

123 Median in typical 'trouser suit' with an overcoat worn in the fashion of a cape

122

123

of a simple cut with tapering legs (figure 122). Over these is worn a thigh length tunic or shirt with long sleeves, again of a fairly simple cut. Some shaping is achieved by use of a belt around the waist and some sculptors indicate folds in the shirt where the material has been pulled in by the belt; from this it can be inferred that the shirts had straight side seams and were not 'fitted'. Over this basic outfit some figures wear long overcoats (figure 123) and although these always have long sleeves they are worn thrown over the shoulder and with the sleeves empty like a cape, even to the extent of being fastened across the chest with ties. The normal Median headgear is a rather shapeless bag-like felt hat ranging from quite squat to more cylindrical forms. Some have ribbons pendent behind.

The reliefs at Persepolis are also valuable for depictions of files of people from the nations subject to the Achaemenid kings bringing tribute. For the most part these wear distinctive costumes. The Elamites wear robes and head bands very similar to those of the Susian guards. The Babylonians have differently draped robes which leave their forearms bare and they wear conical hats with a ribbon or tail pendent from the points very much recalling the *kudurru* of Marduk-apal-iddina. The Assyrians don very simple, plain midi-length tunics held by belts made from four strands of material. They appear to wear head cloths or *keffiyehs* made from the same material as their belts.

There are Ionians in tunics of a wavy fabric (wool?) with a shawl draped over in folds; they wear short boots with just a hint of upturned toes and carry in bolts of cloth as part of their tribute. Lydians wear similar tunics also with a shawl and slightly upturned boots but are distinguished by their banded conical headgear which bends over like a wilting ice cream cone. Bactrians or Parthians can be picked out by their sagging wrinkled trousers whilst Scythians and Armenians wear normal Median trouser suits but have distinctive headgear; the former wear pointed helmets with a neck guard and balaclava-like chin piece, the latter a flattened cap concertina-ed over the front of the head. The Indians have only simple kilts with thick rolled waistbands despite the tribute of gold dust which they present.

Conclusion

The reader may well now be left with the impression that many of the garments of the ancient peoples of the near east were the same or at least very similar. Most do however exhibit some subtle differences from one place, period or people to another and 'accessories' such as hairstyle or headgear very often allow clear cut distinctions to be made between the various peoples. However, those who may wish to 'apply' ancient costume in some way, be it for theatrical, model-making or general design purposes, should consult some of the excellent general works on ancient art and history which are available to gain a better idea of context and background. There is little more repulsive to a near eastern archaeologist than seeing a figure in perfect Sumerian dress for example standing in front of a perfect neo-Assyrian relief holding a Hittite axe!

Index

Aamu 30
Abraham 30
Achaemenid empire 59
Alaça Hüyük 37
Alexander the Great 59
Amenophis II 32
Amenophis III 32
Ammonite ruler 46
Amorites 23, 30, 31, colour plate 3
Arabian desert 41
Arameans 40, 41, 42, 45, 52, colour plate 5
Arbil 48
Archers 52
Armenians 63
Armour, scale 52
Arslan Tash 45
Assur 7, 15, 48
Assurbanipal 54, colour plate 7
Assurnasirpal II 48
Assur-Sharrat 54, 58
Assyria 26, 47
Assyrians 6, 48ff, 59, 63
Assyrian reliefs 37, 45, 48
Auxilliaries 52
Azerbaijan 59

Baal 32
Babylon 23, 59
Babylonia 28, 41, 57
Babylonians 6, 23, 59, 63
Bactrians 63
Barrelin 42
Bedouin 44
Beni Hasan 30
Bible 44
Black Obelisk 45
Bogazkoy 35
Bogazkoy gate 38
Boots 56

Canaanites 31, 42, 45, 47, 60, colour plate 4
Carchemish 38, 40
Cavalry 52
Chariotry 52
Chiton 44
Climate 6
Cotton 8
Croesus 59
Cyrus the Great 59

Damascus 45
Darius I 59

Debir 8
Dumuzi 10
Dur-Kurigalzu 24
Dyeing 8, 9, 47

Eannatum 14, 15, 18
Ecbatana 59
Egypt 30, 47, 48
Elam 59
Elamites 63
Esarhaddon 48, 58
Eunuchs 50
Exodus 44
Eye paint 30
'Ezor 44

Fars 59
Felting 9
Fertile Crescent 6, 7
Fishman 54
Flax 8

Genesis 7
Genies 48, 54, 58
Griffons 48
Gudea 19, 21

Hagorah 44
Hamadan 59
Hammurapi 23
Hasanlu 60
Hattusas 35
Hittites 6, 24, 35, 45, colour plate 5
Homer 47

Immortals 62
Inanna 10
Indians 63
Investiture of Zimri-Lim 28
Ionians 63
Israelites 45

Jehu 45

Kanish 48
Kassites 24, 28, 57
Keffiyeh 45, 63
Khuzistan 59
Kilamuwa 42
Kudurru 24, 25, 26, 28, 40, 63
Kuttonet 44, 45

Lachish, siege of 45, 47
Lagash 14, 19
Lamgi-Mari 18

Leather 8, 15
Linen 8
Lion-man 54
Loom weights 7, 8
Lydia 59
Lydians 63

Malataya 36
Manishtusu 18
Maras 40
Marduk-apla-iddina 28, 40, 63
Marduk-apla-iddina II, 26
Marduk-nadin-akhhe 26
Mari 16ff, 22, 27, 29, colour plate 2
Medes 59, 62
Megiddo 32, 34
Me'il 45
Melishipak 25, 26
Meskalamdug 16, 18
Military costume, Assyrian 52
Mitannians 35
Murex sp. shell 9, 47
Mursilis 24
Musicians 50

Nakedness 7
Nana 25, 26
Napirasu 59
Naqia 58
Naram-Sin 21, 22, 59
New Testament 45
Nimrud 47, 48
Niniveh 48
Ningirsu 10

Officers 52

Parthians 63
Patriarchs 30
Persepolis 59, 63
Persians 59, 61
Phoenician purple 9
Phoenicians 47
Phrygians 37, 42
Pins, dress 15
Polos 57
Priests 58

Ras Shamra 32
Robe of honour 61
Royal Gate 35

Sadin 44
Sakcegozu 42
Sandals 8, 22, 30, 56

Sargon I 10
Sargon II 56, 57
Scribes 50
Scythians 63
Sea Peoples 37, 41, 47
Sennacherib 8, 45, 50, 52
Shalmaneser 45
Shoes 56
Shoes with up-turned toes 36, 38, 45
Sidon 47
Silk 8
Simlah 44, 45
Slingmen 52
Soldiers 31
Spearmen 12, 52, 61-63, colour plates 6 and 8
Spindle whorls 7, 8
Spinning 8, 11
Standard of Ur 11, 13, 14, 15, 16
Stela of Vultures 14, 15, 18
Sumerians 6, 10ff, 59, colour plate 1
Suppiluliuma 35
Susa 60, 62

Tablets 7
Tanners 8
Tell Agrab 16
Tell Asmar 16
Tell Chuera 16, 18
Tell Halaf 47
Thebes 31
Tiglathpileser III 45, 50, 52, 54, 56, 57, 58
Tukulti-Ninurta I 57
Tyre 47

Ugarit 32, 34
Underwear 44
Untashgal 59
Ur 10, 11, 14, 16
Ur-Nanshe 16, 18
Uruk vase 10

Veils 45
Victory Stela 22

Water goddess 24, 29
Wool 8

Yazilikaya 36, 37

Zimri-Lim 28
Zincirli 38, 42, 48